homemade

homemade

Irresistible Homemade Recipes
for Every Occasion

Clodagh McKenna

Photography by Alberto Peroli

KYLE BOOKS

To Erin McKenna
My business partner, best buddy,
and lucky for me married my
brother. You make everything possible...
I can never thank you enough xx

This edition first published in 2014 by
Kyle Books
an imprint of Kyle Cathie Ltd.
192-198 Vauxhall Bridge Road
London, SW1V 1DX
general.enquiries@kylebooks.com
www.kylebooks.com

First published in Great Britain in 2010 by
Kyle Cathie Limited

10 9 8 7 6 5 4 3 2 1

ISBN 978 0 85783 259 7

Project Managed by Blue Dragonfly, www.bluedragonfly-uk.com
(Caroline West, Editorial; Mark Latter, Design)
Photography by Alberto Peroli
Food styling by Clodagh McKenna
Home economy and props styling by Polly Webb-Wilson
Production by Gemma John

Clodagh McKenna is hereby identified as the author of this work in
accordance with Section 77 of the Copyright, Designs and Patents
Act 1988.

A Cataloguing in Publication record for this title is available from
the British Library.

Printed and bound by 1010 Printing, China

Note to Reader
- Metric measures are given within the recipes and imperial
conversions are provided at the back of the book. Make sure that
you use only one set of measurements and not a combination of
them both.
- All spoon measurements are level unless otherwise stated.
- Eggs are medium unless otherwise stated.

contents

introduction

My starting point for this book was the *Housekeeper's Guide* that my Mum was given when she first set up home. She still has it – a huge, heavy book with a hessian cover. It's battered round the edges from constant use, and favourite recipe pages are covered in sticky fingerprints. As a child, I used it for pressing flowers, and occasionally insects, but for my mum it was like a housekeeping bible, stuffed with recipes, handy tips and sound advice.

This book is not just for new brides, but also for single dads, independent women, couples and everyone in between. There are ideas on entertaining, cooking for yourself, friends and family, and organising and decorating your home. The book is packed with handy household tips and advice on everything from table settings to how to select the perfect cheeseboard.

The chapters reflect my own approach to cooking and home-making. I prefer to use foods and flowers that are in season. I am a great believer in maintaining old traditions, such as preserving fruits and vegetables in autumn to use through the winter. I love the informality of a lazy brunch as much as the elegant formality of afternoon tea; I love the sophistication of apéritifs just as much as curling up for a cosy fireside supper. Our lives are very varied: I wanted to reflect this in the chapters, finding food and ideas to suit every mood and occasion.

My aim is for this book to become a kitchen companion to you in the same way that my Mum's housekeeping manual was to her. A faithful friend you can turn to when you need good solid advice on stocking up the larder and on storage, inspiration for dinner-party menus, ideas for something nutritious for a lunchbox, a recipe for jam or maybe even just somewhere you can press fresh flowers!

Clodagh McKenna

I love using seasonal produce like fresh summer raspberries.

Manage the storage space in your kitchen so that the cupboards are never bare or packed with items that are out of date.

I think it's amazing how a certain taste can become special and captivate your heart.

simple everyday

the well-fed larder

preserved

the envied lunchbox

a guide to cheese and wine

the well-fed larder

Hands up anyone who has an out-of-date product in their kitchen cupboards? Keep your hands up if it's over six months out of date...and twelve months?

We all do it: stuff the cupboards full, forget what's at the back, and then buy stuff we've already got. However, a little organisation makes a world of difference. I divide my cupboards into four different areas: oils and vinegars; dried foods (including pasta, flour, rice, pulses, sugar and salt); tinned foods (tomatoes, vegetables, fruit and fish); and jams and preserves. If you're like me, you will have core ingredients that you use all the time; this is your starting point.

Do a monthly cupboard check, or, if you want to be really organised, keep a list on the inside of your cupboard door of what's low and what you need at the next shop.

We don't all have the luxury of a walk-in pantry, but in this chapter I'll show you how to manage the space you have so that your kitchen cupboards will never be bare or packed with stuff that is out of date. You need to be honest about what you do cook, though. There's no point buying exotic ingredients if you don't get round to making the dishes. Start a minimal list and add to it as you go along. Do a monthly cupboard check, or, if you want to be really organised, keep a list on the inside of your cupboard door of what's low and what you need at the next shop.

Cupboard love is good. Have a thorough clean-out. Here are three incentives for doing so: one, it saves you money; two, it means there is always something in the cupboard if you want to whip up a meal in no time; and three, you know that what's in there isn't going to make you unwell.

one

two

three

on the shelf

shelf one:

flours, sugars,
raising agents, etc.

shelf two:

spices, nuts, dried fruits,
oils, vinegars, canned
goods, etc.

shelf three:

pasta, rice, pulses,
noodles, etc.

preserved

I once made a batch of apple jelly and took a jar home to my Dad. As he took off the lid, he became quite emotional. The smell and taste of the jelly, which was exactly like his mum's, had brought a flood of childhood memories rushing back.

I think it's incredible how a taste can get to your heart as well as your taste buds. Last winter I opened a jar of preserved lemons to add to a chicken tagine. As soon as I cut into the fruit, the aroma transported me straight back to the market place in Italy where I'd bought the lemons the summer before. There's something magical about squirreling away the season's surplus fruit and vegetables along with our memories in a glass jar. Preserving is an instinct: it helps us feel a little bit self-sufficient, as though we can provide for our friends and family. Every culture in the world has found ways to do it – lemons in North Africa, vegetables in Italy, walnuts in Iran, jams and chutneys in Ireland. The recipes in this section are from as far afield as North Africa, South America and Italy.

For very little effort, preserves provide a large reward. Maybe that's why they make such good gifts. They look great, they make us feel good, they taste delicious and they evoke powerful memories – that's a lot to store in a glass jar.

tips on preserving

- Only fill each jar to within 0.5cm of the top.

- To test if your jam is set, place a teaspoon of jam on a chilled plate and allow the jam to cool. If it wrinkles the jam is set.

- If you wish to reduce the amount of sugar you use when making jam, substitute half of the quantity with honey.

- For non-liquid foods, it's important to remove any trapped air bubbles from the top of the jar. To do this, skim the top of the preserve with a knife.

- Wash preserving jars well and then sterilise them by placing in a hot oven for about an hour.

fennel and coriander pickled carrots

I made this pickle when I lived in Turin in Italy. The recipe was given to me by Michelle Fuerst, who is known as the 'Pickling Queen' in California. I met her at the Slow Food *Salone del Gusto* (food festival). In Italy these are eaten along with a glass of wine as an apéritif. You can also use a fennel bulb in this recipe.

serves 4

3 large carrots
1 onion

For the brine
250ml cider vinegar
125ml champagne vinegar
750ml water
1 teaspoon sea salt
1 teaspoon sugar
1 teaspoon fennel seeds
1 teaspoon coriander seeds
1 whole dried chilli
12 bay leaves

Peel the carrots and cut them diagonally into pieces, about 3mm thick. Cut the onion in half and slice into moons, about 1cm thick. Set the carrots and onion to one side.

Put all the brine ingredients in a saucepan and bring to the boil over a medium heat, stirring occasionally.

Once at a slow boil, stir in the sliced onion and cook for a further 5 minutes. Remove the onion with a slotted spoon, and set aside to cool.

When the brine is again at a boil, add the carrots and cook for about 5 minutes. Remove the carrots with the slotted spoon and spread them out to cool.

Once the brine and vegetables have cooled, put them in a storage container and refrigerate. The preserved carrots should last for a few weeks in the fridge.

homemade ketchup

I am an official ketchup lover... I am talking about homemade ketchup and if you do take the time to make this recipe, it will be hard for you to go back to the shop-bought version, so there is your warning! Make a big batch every couple of months because it will last in the fridge for that length of time.

makes 1.5 litres

200ml cider vinegar
1 bay leaf
½ teaspoon ground coriander
½ teaspoon ground cinnamon
7 tablespoons demerara sugar
1.5kg ripe tomatoes, quartered and deseeded
1 teaspoon sea salt
1 tablespoon English mustard powder
1 garlic clove, crushed
1 dessertspoon Worcestershire sauce
2 tablespoons tomato purée
½ teaspoon cornflour (if necessary)

Put the vinegar, bay leaf, coriander, cinnamon and sugar in a heavy-bottomed saucepan and bring to a gentle simmer.

Stir in the tomatoes, salt, mustard powder, garlic, Worcestershire sauce and tomato purée, and bring to the boil, stirring every few minutes.

Reduce the heat and simmer for 30 minutes, adding some cornflour to thicken, if necessary.

Remove from the heat and leave to cool for a few minutes. Transfer to a food-processor or liquidiser and blend until smooth. Press the sauce through a sieve into a bowl and leave to cool completely before bottling.

sun-dried tomatoes

If you have a glut of tomatoes at the end of the summer, then drying them is a great way of preserving the taste for the winter. They take a while to dry, but the amount of preparation required is very small.

makes 60

30 tomatoes
2 tablespoons finely chopped
  fresh rosemary
2 tablespoons finely chopped
  fresh thyme
pinch of sea salt

to prepare your tomatoes for drying
Carefully wash and dry the tomatoes.

Cut the tomatoes in half lengthways, removing the seeds if you wish. If you remove the seeds, make sure you do not remove the pulp.

to sun-dry
Place the tomatoes skin-side down on a wire cooling rack.

Sprinkle over the salt and fresh rosemary and thyme.

Place the rack of tomatoes in a hot sheltered spot, such as a conservatory or on a sunny windowsill. Cover with a mesh food cover to keep the flies off.

It will take at least a few days of sunshine – sometimes up to 12 days – for the tomatoes to dry properly.

to oven-dry
Preheat the oven to its lowest setting.

Prepare the tomatoes as above and put the rack of tomatoes in the oven.

Bake for 6–12 hours until the tomatoes are shrivelled and dry.

to store
The best way to store sun-dried tomatoes is in glass jars. Pack the tomatoes tightly in the jars and seal with a tight-fitting lid. Place the jars in a cool dark place in the kitchen or storecupboard and the tomatoes will last for about 1 year.

to rehydrate
Place the tomatoes in a large bowl of water for 2 hours.

cook's tip

making sun-dried tomato pesto

Put 200g of semi sun-dried tomatoes, 80g of freshly grated Parmesan cheese, 150ml of olive oil, 1 garlic clove and 70g of pine nuts into a blender and whizz for 3 minutes or until smooth. Add more olive oil if the pesto is too thick. Pour into a sterilised jar with a tight-fitting lid and store in the fridge. The pesto will last for up to a month.

When I first started making this chutney it was to sell at my stall at the farmers' markets in Cork, Ireland. It was, and still is, the perfect partner to my chicken liver pâté, which I also sold at my stall (see page 112 for my pâté recipe). Both recipes have remained a constant on my food journey, featuring in many of my meals and always on my restaurant menus.

makes 12 x 230ml jars

christmas chutney

large knob of butter
2 onions, sliced
1kg cooking apples,
   peeled, cored and diced
500g brown sugar
10 whole cloves
1 tablespoon chilli powder
2cm piece of fresh ginger,
   peeled and grated
400ml cider vinegar
1 teaspoon sea salt
1 teaspoon freshly ground
   black pepper
1 tablespoon turmeric powder

---

cook's tip

harvest, preserve, give!

Make this chutney at the end of October when apples are plentiful and at their best. It will last for 6 months and gets better with age – as with all of us! Put in pretty Kilner jars and give to friends and family for Christmas.

Melt a large knob of butter in a heavy-bottomed saucepan and add the onions and apples. Stir well, cover, and allow to cook for 5 minutes.

Stir in the sugar, cloves, chilli powder, fresh ginger, cider vinegar, salt and pepper, and turmeric powder. Mix well. Cover the saucepan and leave to simmer over a medium heat for 20 minutes.

Remove the lid, turn down the heat to low and leave to cook for a further 30 minutes or until the apple has broken down and the chutney has turned a rich golden brown colour. Remove from the heat and leave to cool before putting in sterilised jars.

summer fruit jam

I love preserving the taste of summer as we head into the chillier seasons. This gorgeous jam recipe takes about an hour to make, but will give you months of tasty pleasure...

makes approx. 6x250ml jars

1kg raspberries, strawberries
   (cut into quarters) and loganberries
1kg jam sugar
grated zest of 1 lemon

Put all the berries in a heavy-bottomed saucepan over a low heat and leave to simmer for about 15 minutes.

Add the jam sugar and keep stirring until it dissolves completely.

Add the lemon zest. Turn up the heat and bring to the boil. Leave to boil until the jam begins to set.

To test if it is set, place a teaspoon of jam on a cold saucer and leave it to cool. If it wrinkles and feels firm, the jam is adequately set.

Pour the hot jam into sterilised jars and leave to cool.

Cover each jar with a disc of greaseproof or waxed paper and a lid.

Store in a cool dry place for up to 3 months.

fig jam

When I think of fig jam I think of exotic decadence, but I must say it is the easiest of all the preserves to make and if you serve it with a hard mature goat's cheese, it is one of the most delicious preserves.

makes approx. 1x250ml container

250ml water
150g sugar
12 figs, de-stemmed and quartered
grated zest of 1 lemon
juice of ½ lemon
1 cinnamon stick

Pour the water and sugar into a saucepan and place over a medium heat, stirring until the sugar has dissolved.

Add the figs to the sugar mixture along with the lemon zest and juice and the cinnamon stick. Stir and bring to a light simmer, leaving the lid off the saucepan. Cook for about 1 hour or until the mixture has thickened.

Remove from the heat, take out the cinnamon stick and leave to cool.

Store in an airtight container in the fridge for about 3 months.

cook's tips

buying figs

When shopping for figs, make sure that they are ripe – the colour of the skin should be a deep purple and the fruit should yield slightly to pressure. The best place to store figs is in the fridge, as they have an extremely short shelf-life. Then, about an hour before you are planning to cook them, take them out of the fridge to bring the fruit to room temperature.

making and using jam

• Follow the recipe for Summer Fruit Jam (opposite), but use different summer fruits, such as gooseberries or blackberries, instead.

• Sandwich 2 light sponges with some Summer Fruit Jam and lots of cream.

• Make a large batch of Summer Fruit Jam because it will store in sterilised jars for up to 3 months.

lemon curd

I was always a huge fan of lemon curd when I was a child, but it is only recently that I have started enjoying this lemon delight again and I smother everything in it!

makes 1x250ml jar

5 eggs
160g white sugar
100ml lemon juice
60g butter, cut into small pieces
1 tablespoon grated lemon zest

Suspend a glass bowl over a pan of simmering water. Crack in the eggs and add the sugar and lemon juice. Whisk together until blended. Stir constantly for about 10 minutes so that the curd doesn't scramble.

Remove from the heat and push the curd into a bowl through a fine sieve to remove any lumps.

Whisk the butter into the mixture until it has melted and the mixture is smooth.

Add the lemon zest and leave to cool. The lemon curd will thicken as it cools.

Once the curd has cooled, cover immediately and refrigerate for up to a week.

cook's tips

wicked ways with lemon curd

• Spread on toasted brioche bread has to be one of the most heavenly ways of eating lemon curd.

• Make a delicious Victoria sponge cake by sandwiching 2 light sponges with lemon curd and whipped cream (see my recipe for Old-Fashioned Victoria Sponge on page 129 and use some lemon curd rather than jam).

• Folded through crushed meringues with some whipped cream (see my recipe for Little Lemon Meringue Angels on page 179).

• Drizzled over ice cream, shortcake biscuits or scones – is there anything that doesn't taste better with lemon curd?

preserved lemons

I love the sweetness of preserved lemons. When I lived in Italy, there was a market on my piazza and during the summer all the lemons would come up from Amalfi to be sold in boxes. I used to buy a couple of boxes every summer and preserve the lemons for the winter months. They add so much flavour to dishes...

makes 20 preserved lemon wedges

10 unwaxed lemons
9 teaspoons sea salt
10 peppercorns
10 coriander seeds
4 bay leaves
5 cloves
1 cinnamon stick

Cut 5 of the lemons into quarters and remove the pips.

Sprinkle 1 teaspoon of salt into a sterilised jar and then press a layer of the lemon quarters on top. Cover with 2 teaspoons of salt, a couple of peppercorns and coriander seeds, a bay leaf and a clove. Repeat this process until you reach the top of the jar.

Break the cinnamon stick in half and push both halves down the side of the jar.

Juice the remaining 5 lemons and pour the juice into the jar. Seal and place in a cool dark place for 3 weeks before using.

The preserved lemons will last for about 3 months.

using preserved lemons in your cooking

• Dice a preserved lemon and add to 100ml of Greek yogurt and 1 tablespoon of finely chopped fresh mint. Serve with grilled lamb or chicken.

• Dice a preserved lemon and fold through couscous with some feta, black olives, fresh coriander and ground cinnamon and cumin, and lots of olive oil.

• Dice a couple of preserved lemons and mix well with some softened butter, crushed garlic and fresh basil. Then, spread under the skin of a whole chicken and roast as normal.

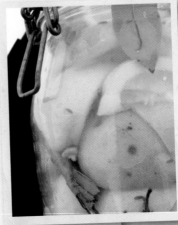

homemade limoncello

Chilled homemade limoncello in the summer – followed by a strong espresso and a chocolate truffle – is one of life's great pleasures.
I usually make about 5 bottles at a time because the limoncello will last for 6 months in a bottle.

makes 1 litre

150ml water
200g caster sugar
grated zest and juice of
   8 unwaxed lemons
700ml vodka

Place a saucepan over a medium heat, add the water and sugar, and stir until the sugar dissolves. Bring to the boil. Reduce the heat and leave to simmer for 3–4 minutes until the liquid is syrupy.

Remove the pan from the heat, add the lemon zest and juice, and leave to cool.

Pour the vodka into the lemon syrup.

Line up the sterilised bottles and pour in the liquid. Leave in a cool dark place for a month, shaking every day for the first week. After a month, the lemon liqueur will be ready to drink. Transfer into clean sterilised bottles.

Before serving, place the limoncello in a freezer for a couple of hours. The limoncello is best served in frozen shot glasses.

raspberry cordial

I love drinking this cordial with sparkling water or adding a few drops to prosecco or cava. You can vary the recipe by replacing the raspberries with blackberries, blueberries or strawberries.

makes 1 litre

250g raspberries
350g sugar
juice of ½ lemon
500ml water

Put the raspberries, sugar, lemon and half the water into a saucepan, and place over a medium heat. Stir and cook for 5 minutes until the raspberries begin to break down.

Stir in the other half of the water, bring to the boil, and then turn down the heat and leave to cook for a further 15 minutes.

Tip the raspberry mixture into a food-processor and whizz until you get a smooth consistency.

Strain into a bowl through a fine sieve using the back of a spoon to push the fruit through the sieve.

Pour into sterilised bottles, seal tightly and store in the fridge for up to 3 weeks.

To serve, dilute 1 part raspberry cordial with 4 parts sparkling water.

the envied lunchbox

Let me ask you a question: why bother with a lunchbox? Maybe because it tastes better than a takeaway sandwich? Or you know it's healthier or it brightens your morning knowing you've got a fabulous lunch to look forward to?

I ask the question because, let's face it, preparing a lunchbox does take a bit of effort, but I really believe it's worth it. You spend all morning dealing with the phone, with emails, with other people. Lunch is your time – this is something you do for yourself, so it needs to be great. Let's take a look at the lunchbox itself. You need sections in the box to separate sweet and savoury, as well as a little tub with a good seal for your pickles and dips. Pack a cloth napkin – it saves on paper – and a small knife for cold meats and fruit. If you're one of those people who falls asleep at the computer after a carby lunch (guilty!), try experimenting with salads or a hearty vegetable soup. If you do a roast on Sunday, put aside some meat and make a delicious couscous for your lunchbox.

I really looked forward to lunch when I worked at farmers' markets because the stall-holders would all swap food. Why not try this at work? Find a lunchbox buddy or even start a lunchbox rota, where one person brings something new in each day. It's great trying new things and makes lunch a really sociable occasion. And, remember, lunch has to be gorgeous as well as good for you, so always pack a treat, like some Chocolate and Hazelnut Drops in this chapter.

tips for packing your children's lunchboxes

make those sandwiches fun

If you decide to pack a traditional sandwich, try cutting the bread into fun shapes using a cookie cutter. You'll be amazed at how a boring cheese sandwich will get gobbled up when shaped into a flower or dinosaur!

make eating fruit fun!

Make colourful skewers with bite-sized pieces of fruit. Kids love smoothies and they are packed with vitamins. Try my Peach and Honey Smoothie on page 44.

dip it!

Kids love dipping stuff. For an easy and nutritious lunch snack, cut vegetables into sticks and serve with a delicious homemade hummus. Try my Pink Hummus on page 176.

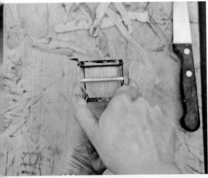

vegetable crisps

Vegetable crisps are a healthy and tasty snack – a really lovely treat to look forward to during the day when you are plodding along at work. They are also a great alternative in children's lunchboxes.

makes 4 small bags of crisps

2 parsnips
2 beetroot
2 sweet potatoes
2 tablespoons olive oil
sea salt and freshly ground black pepper

Preheat the oven to 190°C/gas mark 5.

Peel all the vegetables, using a vegetable peeler or mandolin, and slice them diagonally into wafer-thin crisps. Spread out on a tea-towel or some kitchen paper to remove excess moisture.

Tip all the vegetables into a bowl. Season with salt and pepper, and pour over the olive oil. Toss with your hands to coat evenly.

Arrange the vegetables in a single layer on a baking tray. Roast in the oven on the lowest shelf for 20 minutes, turning them over half way through. Keep an eye on them, as they may not need the full time – they are ready when the parsnips and sweet potatoes are golden brown.

Spread out on kitchen paper until cool and crisp.

the envied lunchbox

spiced butternut squash soup

I love butternut squash soup, especially cooked with these spices. It's also fabulous with smoked bacon or nutmeg. Recently, I was treated to butternut squash soup with roasted porcini mushrooms and crushed hazelnuts – divine.

serves 6

20g butter
500g squash, deseeded and chopped into 2cm pieces
100g onions, chopped
1 garlic clove, crushed
1 tablespoon ground cumin
500ml hot chicken stock
100ml single cream
small bunch of fresh coriander, finely chopped
sea salt and freshly ground black pepper

Melt the butter in a heavy-bottomed saucepan and add the squash, onion and garlic. Cover and leave to simmer for about 15 minutes, stirring occasionally.

Add the ground cumin and sweat for a further 5 minutes.

Stir in the chicken stock and bring the soup to the boil. When the squash is tender (about 10 minutes), stir in the cream and leave to simmer for a minute.

Ladle the soup into a liquidiser and whizz until it reaches a smooth consistency. Season to taste.

Serve hot, stirring in the fresh coriander just before serving.

cook's tip

making stock for soup

• For beef stock, brown marrow bones either by roasting or frying them. When they are browned, add chopped onion, celery and carrots with a whole bulb of garlic, and cover with water. Add a spoonful of tomato purée, a splash of red wine, thyme, a bay leaf and black pepper. Simmer gently for 2 hours.

• For chicken stock, replace the marrow bones with a chicken carcass, the red wine with white wine and the thyme with a bouquet garni.

• For fish stock, add fish bones to vegetables like leek and fennel and flavour with dill or a bouquet garni.

orzo vegetable soup

I started making this delicious soup when I lived in Turin in northern Italy. The winters were fiercely cold there. I craved warm, healthy, comforting dishes, and this one became my weekly lunch companion.

serves 6

2 tablespoons olive oil
1 onion, finely chopped
2 garlic cloves, crushed
1 carrot, peeled and finely chopped
1 celery stalk, finely chopped
1 courgette, finely chopped
800ml hot vegetable stock
400g tin of good-quality tomatoes
400g tin of chickpeas
1 teaspoon dried oregano
100g orzo
sea salt and freshly ground
   black pepper

Place a large saucepan over a medium heat. Pour in the olive oil and then stir in the onion and garlic. Cover and allow to simmer for 2 minutes.

Stir in the carrot, celery and courgette. Cover and leave to cook for a further 5 minutes.

Pour in the vegetable stock, tomatoes and chickpeas. Bring to the boil, then reduce the heat and simmer.

Stir in the dried oregano and orzo, season with salt and pepper, and continue to simmer for about 10 minutes or until the orzo is fully cooked and tender.

cook's tip

making soup

• Save your butter wrappers and use them to cover vegetables when sweating them to make soup.

• Sweat your vegetables for as long as possible because this intensifies the flavour of the soup.

• Cleaned plastic milk bottles are brilliant for freezing soups in.

pea soup with smoked bacon

The frozen peas in this recipe work brilliantly. They are a staple ingredient that you can have to hand in your freezer in order to make this soup in 20 minutes...

serves 6

knob of butter
1 potato, peeled and diced
1 onion, diced
3 strips of smoked streaky bacon, diced
800ml hot chicken stock
450g frozen peas
100ml double cream
2 tablespoons finely chopped fresh mint
50ml crème fraîche
sea salt and freshly ground black pepper
a few mint leaves, to garnish

Melt the butter in a heavy-bottomed saucepan over a medium heat and add the potato and onion. Reduce the heat, stir, cover and leave to sweat for 5 minutes.

Remove the lid, turn the heat up a little and stir in two-thirds of the bacon. Leave to cook for a further 3 minutes.

Pour in the chicken stock and leave the vegetables to simmer for 5 minutes.

Tip in the frozen peas and cook for 5 minutes.

While the peas are cooking, place a frying pan over a high heat, tip in the remaining bacon, and cook for a couple of minutes or until the bacon is nice and crispy. Set aside in a bowl.

Season the soup with salt and pepper, and then blend in a liquidiser.

Stir in the cream and mint.

Pour the hot soup into warmed bowls. Using a teaspoon, add a few drops of crème fraîche to the soup in each bowl, followed by a sprinkle of the fried bacon and a mint leaf.

Delicious!

cook's tip

keeping soup green!

Don't cover the soup once you have added the peas, as it will dull the bright green colour. This goes for all green-coloured vegetable soups like spinach and broccoli.

lip-smacking sandwiches

These are a few of my favourite sandwiches. Wrap them in greaseproof paper in your lunchbox, or if you are going on a picnic, as I find that clingfilm can make them a little soggy.

fresh tuna salad

I always feel so healthy after eating this sandwich. If you are trying to cut down on carbs, then don't use any bread and simply eat as a salad instead.

makes 2 rolls

150g good-quality tinned tuna, drained
½ apple, cored and grated
½ celery stick, finely sliced
1 tablespoon mayonnaise
grated zest and juice of 1 lemon
4 leaves of iceberg lettuce (or another crispy variety)
sea salt and freshly ground black pepper
2 good-quality brown rolls

Pop the tuna, apple, celery, mayonnaise, lemon juice and zest in a bowl. Season with salt and pepper, and mix well.

Cut open the rolls, line them with the lettuce and scoop the tuna salad mix on top.

smoked salmon with sun-dried tomatoes

It makes such a difference if you use good-quality smoked salmon when making this delicious sandwich.

makes 2 sandwiches

2 dessertspoons mayonnaise
4 slices of sourdough bread
10 semi sun-dried tomatoes
12 capers
4 slices of smoked salmon
sea salt and freshly ground black pepper

Spread the mayonnaise over the 4 slices of bread.

Arrange the sun-dried tomatoes and capers on 2 slices of the bread and lay the smoked salmon slices on top.

Season with salt and pepper, and cover with the other 2 slices of bread. Cut in half and enjoy!

new york reuben

Whenever I am in New York City, I go to the famous 'Katz' and devour one of their amazing Reubens (they do the best in the city). This recipe is the closest I have come to recreating the sandwich in Ireland. The Russian dressing used in this recipe can be made at home or bought in bottles from most good food stores.

makes 2 sandwiches

1 tablespoon grainy Dijon mustard
4 slices rye bread
200g corned beef, thinly sliced
100g Swiss cheese, thinly sliced
200g sauerkraut, drained
80ml Russian dressing (see below)
50g butter (optional, for grilling)

For the Russian dressing
80g mayonnaise
1 teaspoon Worcestershire sauce
1 teaspoon tomato ketchup
1 teaspoon mustard

Spread the mustard on 2 slices of the rye bread. Divide the corned beef between the bread slices, followed by the cheese and sauerkraut. Spread the Russian dressing over the other 2 slices of bread and place on top of the first 2 slices of bread.

You can also grill a Reuben sandwich on a griddle pan, which is a more authentic way of making it. Melt the butter on the griddle pan. When it has melted, put the prepared sandwiches in the pan and toast both sides.

crispy bacon, creamy avocado and sweet tomato sambo

Crispy, creamy, sweet and crunchy – utter heaven in a bite! Make sure you use a good-quality, smoked, streaky bacon – I use Gubbeen bacon from a farm in West Cork in Ireland.

makes 2 sandwiches

6 slices of streaky bacon
sunflower oil, for frying
1 ripe avocado, sliced
8 sweet cherry tomatoes, halved
4 slices of good-quality white bread
freshly ground black pepper

Fry the bacon in a drop of sunflower oil in a medium to hot frying pan. Cook until the bacon is crispy on both sides. Alternatively, cook under a hot grill.

Arrange the avocado on 2 slices of bread, followed by the cherry tomatoes and streaky bacon. Season with pepper, cover with the other 2 slices of bread, and cut in half.

asparagus and gruyère tart

The asparagus in this tart is tops for me, but I have also used thinly sliced broccoli and feta instead of the Gruyère, and that combination also works an absolute treat.

serves 6

For the pastry
60g chilled butter, diced
120g plain flour
approx. 50ml water

For the filling
300g asparagus spears
3 eggs, beaten
60g grated Gruyère
250ml single cream
8 fresh basil leaves
sea salt and freshly ground black pepper

Start by making the pastry. Use your fingertips to rub the butter into the flour, then add enough cold water to bring the pastry dough together. Wrap in clingfilm and put in the fridge to cool for 30 minutes.

Preheat the oven to 180°C/gas mark 4.

Once the pastry has chilled, roll it out using a wooden rolling pin and line a 19cm flan tin, pressing the dough down firmly and trimming off the excess pastry around the edge of the tin. Bake in the oven for 15 minutes.

While the pastry is baking, cook the asparagus by simmering in a small pan of salted water for 3 minutes. Drain and slice the spears in half.

Beat together the eggs, cheese and cream, and season with salt and black pepper.

Pour the egg mixture into the tart and arrange the asparagus spears and fresh basil leaves on top.

Bake the tart at the same temperature for a further 30 minutes or until the centre feels firm and looks golden brown.

cook's tip

easy pastry rolling

An easy way to roll out your pastry is to place your dough on a sheet of clingfilm and then lay another one on top. Using your rolling pin, roll out the pastry. The clingfilm stops the dough from sticking to your work surface and also from breaking up as you roll.

tuscan-style marinated chicken with almond, apricot and feta couscous

The first time that I tasted this recipe was at a wedding on an olive estate in Tuscany. The day after the wedding, they organised a huge barbecue and served this marinated chicken. It's delicious... and I couldn't leave without a copy of the recipe! It works just as well with pork and lamb, too. You might also like to try combining the chicken with my Moroccan-Spiced Couscous and Chickpea Salad (see page 42).

serves 4

2 chicken breasts, free-range or organic if possible

For the marinade
250ml olive oil
5 tablespoons balsamic vinegar
1 tablespoon finely chopped rosemary
2 garlic cloves, crushed
sea salt and freshly ground black pepper

For the couscous
200g couscous
70g dried apricots, diced
350ml hot chicken stock
2 tablespoons lemon juice
3 tablespoons extra virgin olive oil
50g flaked almonds, toasted
100g baby spinach
50g feta, crumbled
sea salt and freshly ground black pepper

Place the chicken and all the marinade ingredients in a large bowl and mix well. Cover and put in the fridge, and leave to marinate for up to 12 hours.

Preheat the oven to 180°C/gas mark 4.

Remove the chicken, place on a hot griddle pan, and season. Cook on each side for 2 minutes before placing in the preheated oven for 10 minutes.

Meanwhile, put the couscous in a large bowl with the apricots, season with salt and black pepper, and mix well. Pour the chicken stock over the couscous and cover immediately with a large plate or cling film to seal in the steam. Leave for 10 minutes.

Fluff up the couscous with a fork to separate the grains and stir in the lemon juice, olive oil, almonds, baby spinach and feta.

Once the chicken is cooked, cut into thin strips, leave to cool, and fold into the couscous.

moroccan-spiced couscous and chickpea salad

It's simple to make, full of fibre and very low in fat. It will last for about 3 days, so is a great salad to make on a Sunday night for lunch on Monday and Tuesday. It can also be used as a sandwich filler with soft goats' cheese.

serves 4

200g couscous
40g raisins
1 teaspoon ground cumin
1 teaspoon ground coriander
½ teaspoon ground cinnamon
350ml hot chicken stock
100g good-quality tinned chickpeas, rinsed and drained
2 tablespoons lemon juice
3 tablespoons extra virgin olive oil
½ red onion, finely diced
2 tablespoons freshly chopped flat-leaf parsley
sea salt and freshly ground black pepper

Put the couscous in a large bowl with the raisins and spices, season with salt and pepper, and mix well. Pour the chicken stock over the couscous and cover immediately with a large plate or cling film to seal in the steam. Set aside for 10 minutes.

Fluff up the couscous with a fork to separate the grains and stir in the chickpeas, lemon juice, olive oil, red onion and parsley.

summer rice salad

This northern Italian salad is super-healthy and often serves as my supper.

serves 2

100g rice (basmati or wild)
70g sweetcorn
70g frozen peas or French beans
100g cherry tomatoes, halved
2 hard-boiled eggs
glug of extra virgin olive oil
juice of 1 lemon
sea salt and freshly ground black pepper

Rinse the rice and tip into a pan of boiling water. Cook for 15–20 minutes. Rinse again with cold water and leave to cool.

If using frozen peas tip them into a saucepan of boiling water and allow to simmer for 5 minutes, then drain and rinse under cold water. Once the rice has cooled, put it in a large bowl and mix in the sweetcorn, peas and cherry tomatoes.

Cut the hard-boiled eggs into quarters, then halve again and toss into the rice.

Add the extra virgin olive oil and lemon juice. Season with salt and pepper, and mix well.

banana bread

This delicious recipe can also be used to make muffins. Try adding chopped pecan nuts and walnuts to the recipe. The banana bread will last all week, so is an excellent sweet bread to make for those afternoon treats that we all need!

makes 1 loaf

125g butter, plus extra for greasing
150g light soft brown sugar
2 eggs, beaten
3 very ripe bananas, mashed
250g plain flour
1 tablespoon baking powder
½ teaspoon grated nutmeg
pinch of sea salt

Preheat the oven to 180°C/gas mark 4.

Grease a 1kg loaf tin and line the base with baking parchment.

Beat the butter and sugar together until fluffy and pale in colour.

Add the eggs, a little at a time, beating well after each addition. Add the bananas to this mixture.

Sift the dry ingredients together and then fold gently into the banana mixture. (It is important to fold the dry ingredients in gently until they are just incorporated, rather than simply stirring.)

Transfer the mixture to the prepared tin and bake for 50–60 minutes or until a skewer placed in the middle of the cake comes out clean and dry.

Turn out onto a wire rack to cool.

peach and honey smoothie

Every day I try to drink a smoothie. I find that it gives me a boost when I am feeling a little bit sluggish...You can use blueberries, strawberries or raspberries instead of the peaches, if you wish.

makes 1

150g fresh peaches, peeled and sliced
½ banana
1 dessertspoon honey
200ml plain yogurt
4 ice cubes

Place all the ingredients in a liquidiser and whizz until smooth.

oliver's smoothie

Oliver McCabe owns a fabulous food store and café in Ireland called 'Select Stores' in Dalkey, County Dublin. His 'Ladies' Smoothie' is full of the minerals that women need every day, such as calcium, magnesium and vitamin C. I always feel like I am bursting with energy after his juice; it's fabulous!

makes 2

small bunch of parsley
5 small apples
small bunch of alfalfa sprouts
1 ripe whole mango
1 ripe banana
1 teaspoon organic light tahini
1 dessertspoon organic local honey
ice cubes (optional)

Put the parsley and apples in a juicer and juice. Pour the juice into a liquidiser with the rest of the ingredients, then blend for 20 seconds. Add ice if you wish to make the smoothie cooler.

making smoothies

• As fruit tends to deteriorate quite quickly, it is best to freeze berries in bags when you buy them because this also means that you don't have to add in any ice cubes when blitzing.

• If you are trying to cut down on sugar, use honey as an alternative.

• To prevent your liquidiser locking up when making juices or smoothies, add the liquid first and then the solid food.

• If you are freezing smoothies, make sure you leave extra space in your container as they will expand when frozen.

• Mangoes are great for making smoothies sweeter.

crunchy-topped yogurt pots

Yogurt's health credentials are pretty impressive: it boosts the immune system, prevents yeast infections, lowers bad cholesterol and raises good cholesterol. Because it is rich in calcium, it is good for building bones, and it has been found to have a preventative and curative effect on arthritis. Because it kills the bacteria on your tongue, it can help prevent bad breath. Many people also find it eases ulcers and colitis.

makes 4 yogurt jars

50g hazelnuts
50g whole almonds
350g Greek yogurt
80g sultanas
1 teaspoon ground cinnamon

Lightly toast the nuts in a frying pan over a medium heat for about 3 minutes, tossing every 30 seconds or so to make sure that the nuts are toasted evenly.

Fill the jars three-quarters full with yogurt. Place the toasted nuts, sultanas and cinnamon in a bowl and mix well. Spoon the mixture on top of the yogurt.

chocolate and hazelnut drops

I spent two days perfecting this recipe – the cookie crumbles in your mouth and carries just enough chocolate and hazelnuts to make it into the perfect-bite category!

makes 24

250g butter, softened
120g caster sugar
300g plain flour
1 teaspoon baking powder
80g good-quality dark chocolate drops, minimum 70% cocoa solids
70g hazelnuts, roughly chopped

Preheat the oven to 180°C.

Put the butter and sugar in a large bowl and cream together with a wooden spoon until pale in colour.

Sift in the flour and baking powder, and then add the chocolate drops and hazelnuts. Bring the mixture together to form a dough.

Using your hands, roll the dough into small drops and place them slightly apart on two baking trays (there is no need to grease or line).

Flatten the drops slightly with the back of a damp fork and bake in the oven for 13–15 minutes or until they are light golden brown and slightly firm on the top.

Carefully transfer the drops to a wire rack to cool.

cook's tip

crushing hazelnuts

Lay a tea-towel on your work surface, spread out the hazelnuts on the top half of the towel, and cover with the bottom half. Using a rolling pin, forcefully tap the covered hazelnuts. This is an excellent stress-buster, as well as an effective nut-buster!

a guide to cheese and wine

If you're like me, you always keep something in your store cupboard that you can throw together for a quick meal.

I think of the cheese container in my fridge as an extension of the store cupboard. A good airtight container with a choice of cheeses is an absolute godsend. Cheese is fantastic for quick meals, handy as a snack, and great if people pop round unexpectedly.

I change the cheeses I buy every couple of weeks or so, as there are so many wonderful cheeses to try. I like to take a piece of cheese that I have bought from a local farmers' market or deli when I go out to dinner because people really enjoy hearing about the origins of the cheese.

I prefer to serve cheese with water biscuits because it doesn't detract from the flavour of the cheeses as much. I also serve peeled apples, rather than grapes, to cleanse the palate between cheeses. I also serve chutneys with hard cheese. My Christmas Chutney (see page 18) or my Fig Jam (see page 21) would be superb.

Types of cheese

It's useful to understand the different groups of cheese. If you are offered a cheese board in a restaurant, it should include a hard cheese, a semi-hard cheese, a soft cheese, a fresh cheese and a blue cheese.

hard cheese (e.g. Cheddar, Parmigiano Reggiano). Good for cooking and lasts for ages. Hard cheese has the highest fat content and can be oily when melted. A good hard cheese has a tangy flavour.

semi-hard cheese (e.g. Gruyère, Emmenthal, Gouda). This lasts about 3–4 weeks in the fridge and is good for cooking because it isn't too oily or rubbery.

soft cheese (e.g. Camembert, Brie). This needs to be eaten within a few days of purchase and is best served fully ripe and at room temperature.

fresh cheese (e.g. Ricotta, Mozzarella, Cottage Cheese, Boursin). This is made in two ways: either by curdling milk with an enzyme, draining off the whey, and then moulding the remaining curds into cheese or by dropping the curds into hot whey or brine and kneading it, as is the case with mozzarella and burrata.

Fresh cheeses have a reputation for being mild, although this depends on the cheese. For this reason, they often become the vehicle for stronger flavours like herbs or fruits. In fact, they make fantastic, fast, easy meals all on their own. They are also high in protein and calcium, and contain less fat than hard cheese.

Because fresh cheeses don't contain preservatives, they go off quickly and should be eaten as close to the day they were made as possible. When you buy them, there should be no mould and they should smell like fresh milk. Keep them in the fridge and stick to the sell-by-date.

Ricotta and mascarpone are ideal for making trifle or cheese cakes, but they also make a tasty pasta dish added at the last minute with a handful of chopped herbs to a freshly made tomato sauce. Even easier, just add a dollop of ricotta to freshly drained pasta with sautéd mushrooms. Stir in some tarragon and grate over some Irish Desmond or Parmesan cheese. Serve with a crisp white wine and a green salad – a sophisticated meal that won't take you much more than 10 minutes to prepare.

So, let's stop thinking of fresh cheese as something we disguise in puddings, cakes and pizza. Don't trifle with it; give it a new lease of life in your main dishes.

blue cheese (e.g. Stilton, Gorgonzola, Cashiel Blue). Veined cheese injected with mould. Works well in salads or with fruit such as pears. Blue cheese is made by milling the curds and thrusting them into moulds, which are then hand-turned on a daily basis. After 5 weeks, the cheese goes into a blueing machine, a drumful of spikes then pierce it to let in oxygen, which kickstarts the mould that makes the veins.

using buffalo mozzarella

A popular fresh cheese is mozzarella. If you want to taste the real thing – and trust me you'll never look back – buy Mozzarella di Bufala Campana, a DOP designation (Denomination of Protected Origin) for mozzarella made from buffalo milk produced in Campania, Italy. The texture is not rubbery, but creamy, the flavour is sweet and it tastes sublime with vine-ripened tomatoes, fresh basil and a drizzle of olive oil. I also like to tear the mozzarella into pieces and serve it with slices of Parma ham and ripe peaches. Burrata is similar to mozzarella, having both mozzarella and cream inside, which gives it a uniquely soft texture.

recommended goats' cheeses

When young, goats' cheese is mild and creamy. As it gets older, it hardens and has a sharper, more acidic, taste. Ageing gives cheese depth and intensifies the flavour. You will see goats' cheese wrapped in leaves (perhaps soaked in wine or brandy) or rolled in chilli or herbs to impart flavour. Goats' cheese may also be covered in ash to pull out the moisture. Good goats' cheeses include:

From France Crottin de Chavignol, a Pur Chèvre (made only from goats' milk), from the Loire is a soft, crumbly cheese, with a slightly nutty flavour, which is at its best at about 4 weeks. Fantastic grilled and served on a green salad with a white wine such as Pouilly Fumé or Sauvignon Blanc.
From Italy Robiola di Roccaverano, a raw or pasteurised cheese made in the provinces of Asti and Alessandria. A soft cheese with no rind and a delicate, slightly sweet taste.
From Spain Cabra del Tietar, a hard cheese with a long nutty finish that is great with Pinot Noir or even sherry.
From England Little Wallop (by Juliet Harbutt and Alex James of Blur) is washed in cider brandy and wrapped in vine leaves. Ready at 3 weeks, it has an appley flavour with a mushroomy aroma and is great with Riesling or Sauvignon Blanc.
From Ireland Bluebell Falls (by Paul Keane) has a creamy, nutty, caramel flavour that can hold its own with any of the great pecorino cheeses. Try with a Sauvignon Blanc or even a Pinot Noir.

food for family and friends

sweet, sticky and devilishly good

a breakfast frittata cooked in one pan couldn't be simpler.

homemade beans on hot buttered toast must be the ultimate comfort food.

decorating with flowers

It's a wet Dublin day. I open my sitting-room door to be wowed by a splash of sunshine in a vase: my daffodils have opened overnight. They are so vibrant, so impossibly pretty that I can't help but feel happy. Now, those daffodils only cost a few pounds; that's a disproportionate amount of pleasure for so little cost. Freshly cut flowers are like the smell of fresh coffee or baking bread. They turn the house into a home. They are also a great way to express yourself, so be creative and use whatever you have around you.

Any watertight container works as a vase. I use mismatched containers such as medicine jars or old milk jugs with my vases, but use one type of flower throughout the house. It makes more of a statement. Also, if you're given a large bunch of one type of flowers, break them up and display them in a row rather than plonking them all in one vase. It has more impact, particularly with large blooms like chrysanthemums.

I also have a ribbon drawer where I save ties and bows from presents or chocolates. I tie them around vases for an extra dash of colour or to add a touch of zing to the display. A final word: buy flowers when they are in season. It's when they're at their most beautiful and gives us something new to look forward to as the seasons change.

the lazy brunch

Weekdays, I'm usually rushing out of the door with a slice of toast and a mobile clamped to my ear. So, when it comes to the weekend, there is nothing I like more than waking up when I'm ready and having a lazy brunch.

I love the relaxed informality and flexibility of brunch. It can take place any time from mid-morning to mid-afternoon. When I was at college in the United States, I picked up some great tips on lazy, laid-back brunches. Serving brunch buffet-style, for example, means that you don't have to be a short-order cook and can offer plenty of variety. You can't go wrong with a classic egg dish such as Eggs Florentine, while pancakes and muffins are easy to prepare ahead of time and always popular. I also like to serve something sweet with the savoury dishes. My favourite sweet dish is Cinnamon French Toast with Honey Vanilla Mascarpone.

Ideally, a brunch stretches itself out over a few hours, so there is time for fruit juice and coffee first. Drinks are vital: the coffee has to be good-quality, the fruit juices fresh and any alcohol chilled. After a hectic week, brunch is a casual affair, preferably eaten in your pyjamas. The only brunch rule is that there are no rules – just sit back, enjoy your coffee, and keep it coming!

croque madame

My favourite place to eat Croque Madame or Monsieur (the difference being that the Monsieur is a closed sandwich while the Madame is open) is in Café de Flore in St. Germain, in Paris. It's a very simple, bistro-style café where the great artists and writers of Paris would come to share their thoughts.

serves 2

4 slices of sourdough white bread
15g butter
2 slices of cooked ham
1 tablespoon Dijon mustard
6 tablespoons grated Gruyère
sea salt and freshly ground black pepper

Place the sliced bread under a grill and toast one side. Remove from the grill and butter the non-toasted side.

Place half a slice of ham and a smear of Dijon mustard on each slice of bread.

Top with equal amounts of grated Gruyère, then season with salt and pepper.

Pop back underneath the grill until the cheese has melted.

.... cook's tip ....

a perfect poached egg

There is a very simple trick to this – make sure that your water is salted and on a rolling boil. Then, with a spoon, swirl the water and crack the egg as closely to the water as possible (without burning your fingers). You will instantly see the white of the egg cover the yolk. You must also make sure that the eggs are fresh.

classic eggs florentine

cook's tip

a perfect boiled egg

Add a little sprinkle of salt to the water and make sure that the water is boiling and covers the egg by an inch. Then the timings! You will need to boil your egg for 3 minutes for a really soft-boiled yolk, 4 minutes for a slightly set yolk, 5 minutes for a firmer yolk, 6 minutes for hard-boiled with a slightly soft yolk, and 8 minutes for firmly hard-boiled.

Every time I visit New York City, I pass by Sunday brunch at 'Balthazar'. Their Eggs Florentine are so good; they serve the dish with sliced artichokes as well as spinach. Hollandaise is usually a tricky sauce to make because it can split, but try my way of making it in a food-processor, and I promise you that it will be absolute perfection!

serves 2

sunflower oil, for frying
4 slices of smoked streaky bacon
4 freerange or organic eggs
50g butter
150g spinach, with stalks removed

For the Hollandaise sauce
100g butter
2 egg yolks
juice of 1 lemon
sea salt and freshly ground
   black pepper

Place a frying pan over a medium heat, add a drop of oil and fry off the bacon until it is golden brown and crispy. Once cooked, place in a low-heated oven to keep warm.

To make the Hollandaise sauce, first melt the butter in a saucepan. While the butter is melting, pour the egg yolks into a food-processor, followed by the lemon juice. Turn on the food-processor to a medium speed, and slowly pour the melted butter through the feed tube until the butter and egg yolks are thoroughly combined and the sauce has a thick consistency. Season with salt and pepper.

For the poached eggs, place a saucepan of salted water over a high heat and, once the water has come to the boil, give the water a good swirl with a spoon. (Swirling the water helps the white of the egg to form around the yolk.) Bring the eggs, one at a time, as close to the boiling water as possible and crack quite quickly into the water. Reduce the heat to medium and leave to cook for 3 minutes.

While the eggs are poaching, place a frying pan over a high heat and melt the butter. Stir in the spinach and cook until the leaves are wilted.

Arrange the wilted spinach on 2 warmed plates. Place 2 poached eggs on each plate. Pour over the Hollandaise sauce and place the smoked bacon on top. Serve with toast.

full breakfast frittata

This recipe is just superb for when you are cooking brunch for a large number. It will take you about 20 minutes to prepare, but once it is cooked, it can be left to sit in a preheated oven while you get the coffee made.

serves 4

8 freerange or organic eggs
4 tablespoons olive oil
1 onion, sliced
150g potatoes, peeled and diced
4 sausages, cut into 2cm pieces
100g smoked bacon lardons
8 cherry tomatoes, halved
sea salt and freshly ground
   black pepper

Crack the eggs into a large bowl, season with salt and pepper, and whisk lightly.

Place a 30cm frying pan over a medium heat and pour in 3 tablespoons of the olive oil. When the oil is hot, tip in the onion and potatoes, reduce the heat and leave to cook for 10 minutes, stirring every few minutes.

Once the potatoes and onion are cooked, add them to the bowl of whisked eggs, season with salt and pepper, and mix together.

Place the frying pan back on a low heat, add another tablespoon of olive oil, tip in the sausages and bacon lardons, and cook for 5 minutes. Add to the egg mixture.

Put the frying pan back on the heat and, if necessary, pour in a small dollop of olive oil. Pour in the egg mixture. Leave to cook for about 10 minutes or until the egg mixture has set.

Arrange the halved cherry tomatoes on top.

Pop the frittata under a grill for 5 minutes or until it is golden in colour.

cook's tip

tempting alternatives

Try substituting the smoked bacon and sausages for smoked salmon and soft goats' or ricotta cheese. I've also made a delicious Spanish version using chorizo and manchego cheese.

baked eggs

This must be the most simple and scrumptious way to cook eggs. When baking the eggs, make sure that you bake only one or two in a dish at a time because the eggs on the outside get overcooked if you cook more than that.

serves 2

25g butter
4 freerange or organic eggs
50g Gruyère cheese (or another hard cheese such as Cheddar or Gouda), grated
1 teaspoon mustard
1 tablespoon double cream
sea salt and freshly ground black pepper
slices of bread, to serve

Preheat the oven to 180°C/gas mark 4.

Grease 2 small ovenproof dishes with the butter and crack 2 eggs into each one.

Put the cheese in a small bowl and mix in the mustard and cream. Season with salt and pepper. Scoop the cheese mixture on top of the eggs and bake in the oven for 10 minutes.

Serve with toasted bread cut into thin slices so that you can dip them into the eggs.

variations

Add 70g of smoked bacon lardons to the cheese mixture.

Omit the cream mixture and place 4 thin slices of spicy chorizo on top of the eggs.

Wilt 70g of baby spinach in a frying pan with some butter, and bed the dishes with the spinach before you crack in the eggs.

Try sprinkling some breadcrumbs on top of the cheese mixture to get a nice crispy finish.

-------- cook's tip --------

keep it fresh

You can test to see if an egg is fresh by dropping it into a bowl of cold water. If the egg stays at the bottom of the bowl, then it is fresh.

homemade beans on toast

3 shallots, thinly sliced
1 garlic clove, crushed
olive oil, for frying
200g tomato passata
2 tablespoons cider vinegar
1 tablespoon golden syrup
  or dark muscovado sugar
200g cooked cannellini beans
sea salt and freshly ground black pepper

Homemade beans are best made the day before. I also love adding two teaspoons of medium curry powder. They will last in the fridge for 1 week after you make them.

serves 4

Put the shallots and garlic in a casserole dish over a medium heat and sweat in a drop of olive oil for 2–3 minutes.

Stir in the tomato passata, vinegar and syrup (or sugar), season with salt and pepper, and leave to simmer for 5 minutes.

Stir the cannellini beans into the tomato mixture, cover and leave to cook for 70–80 minutes, stirring occasionally. Serve on hot buttered toast.

macedonian fruit salad

2 bananas
1 peach
1 apple
1 kiwi fruit
1 orange
10 grapes
200ml water
juice of 1 lemon
1 teaspoon caster sugar (optional)

Even though I have put this fruit salad in the brunch section, it's a fabulous recipe to make for snacking through the day too. I picked up this recipe while living in Italy.

serves 4

Peel and slice all of the fruit and place in a large bowl. Pour in the water and lemon juice, and mix well. Have a taste; if all the fruit is ripe, you shouldn't have to add any sugar, but sprinkle over some caster sugar if it's lacking in sweetness.

Cover and put in the fridge to marinate for an hour before serving.

cinnamon french toast with honey-vanilla mascarpone

French Toast is my all-time favourite brunch dish, especially when it is made with brioche...If you don't have any brioche, then just use good-quality white bread. If you aren't a fan of cinnamon, then try some freshly grated nutmeg. At my café, we also serve this with crispy streaky bacon.

makes 4

For the French toast
150ml milk
4 eggs
2 teaspoons ground cinnamon
8 slices of brioche
50g butter

For the honey-vanilla mascarpone cream
200ml mascarpone
2 tablespoons honey
½ teaspoon vanilla extract

Put the milk, eggs and cinnamon in a bowl and beat well. Soak the brioche slices in the milk-and-egg mixture for a couple of minutes.

While the slices of brioche are soaking, put the mascarpone cream, honey and vanilla extract in a bowl, and mix together well.

Melt the butter in a frying pan and fry the egg-soaked slices of brioche over a medium heat until they are a golden colour on each side.

Serve the French toast with a dollop of the mascarpone cream.

new-york-style blueberry pancakes

These pancakes are great for serving when you have children to feed for brunch, as they all love pancakes. You can substitute the blueberries with raspberries or chocolate drops if you wish. Make the batter up the night before, so your brunch can remain as relaxed as possible...

makes 10 pancakes

200g self-raising flour
1 tablespoon baking powder
70g caster sugar
1 egg
300ml milk
100g butter (50g melted)
250g fresh blueberries
maple syrup, to serve

To make the pancake batter, sift the flour, baking powder and sugar into a large bowl.

In a separate bowl, whisk the egg and milk together.

Make a well in the centre of the flour mixture, pour in the milk-and-egg mixture and whisk together until you have a smooth creamy consistency. Place in the fridge for a minimum of 1 hour.

Just before cooking the pancakes, stir in the melted butter (or a tablespoon of vegetable oil), which prevents the pancakes from sticking to the pan, and the fresh blueberries.

Over a medium heat, melt a knob of butter in a 12-inch non-stick frying pan, making sure that the butter spreads out all over the base of the pan to form a film.

Spoon 4 tablespoons of batter into the pan. You should be able to fit 3 pancakes at a time on the pan, but remember to leave space in between each one. When you see bubbles forming on the surface of the batter, turn over the pancake and continue to cook on the other side until it is a light golden colour.

As you make them, put the cooked pancakes onto a warm plate covered with tin foil in a low-heated oven.

When you have cooked all of your pancakes, place them on a warmed plate and serve with the maple syrup.

very berry muffins

I make these muffins with buttermilk as I think it adds more flavour, but you can also use normal milk. Having said that, pick up a pint or two of buttermilk if you see it, as it lasts in the fridge for about a month.

makes 12 muffins

400g plain flour
170g caster sugar
1 tablespoon baking powder
finely grated zest of 1 orange
pinch of sea salt
280ml buttermilk
2 eggs, beaten
80g butter, melted
250g blackberries, blueberries or raspberries

Preheat the oven to 200°C/gas mark 6.

Grease a 12-hole muffin tin and set aside.

Mix the flour, sugar, baking powder, orange zest and salt in a large bowl.

In a separate bowl, mix together the buttermilk, eggs and melted butter. Make a well in the centre of the flour mixture and pour in the buttermilk mixture, mixing all the time until the mixture is quite stiff.

Fold in the berries of your choice and fill the muffin cups with the mixture.

Bake in the oven for 15 minutes. Remove from the oven once the muffins have risen and are a golden colour on top. Turn out onto a cooling rack and leave to cool.

cook's tip

other muffin ideas

To make chocolate muffins, subsitute the berries with 150g of good-quality dark chocolate drops. For cranberry muffins, substitute the berries with 200g of dried cranberries.

homemade muesli

I usually prepare five times the quantity of this recipe when I am making muesli and then store it in large Kilner jars. It's fabulous in the morning sprinkled over yogurt or porridge. You can also try adding a teaspoon of ground cinnamon.

makes 12 servings

300g jumbo oats
100g dried figs
100g dried apricots
70g dried cranberries
180g mixed nuts
  (almonds, hazelnuts, walnuts)
50g pumpkin seeds
50g sunflower seeds

Preheat the oven to 190°C/gas mark 5.

Spread out the oats over the base of a large roasting tin and roast in the oven for 15 minutes or until golden in colour. Put the roasted oats in a large bowl and leave to cool.

Roughly chop the dried fruits and nuts. Put the seeds and chopped fruits and nuts in the bowl. Mix well.

Transfer to a seal-proofed container and serve for breakfast with some natural yogurt or milk.

pecan swirls

Sweet, sticky and devilishly good – just make sure that you make enough of these swirls for everyone, as they tend to disappear very fast!

makes 16

For the dough
450g plain flour
50g caster sugar
1 teaspoon sea salt
85g chilled unsalted butter, diced
7g fresh yeast
2 eggs
150ml milk

For the filling
100g pecan nuts
85g brown sugar
2 teaspoons ground cinnamon
a little melted butter for brushing

For the topping
100g pecan nuts, chopped
125g butter, melted
50g brown sugar
125ml maple syrup

Put the flour, sugar and salt in a large bowl and rub in the butter with your fingertips until the mixture resembles breadcrumbs.

Activate the yeast by mixing in a sprinkle of caster sugar using the back of a teaspoon until the yeast becomes liquidy. Whisk the yeast into the milk, followed by the eggs and then pour the milk mixture into the dry ingredients. Mix well.

Tip the dough onto a lightly floured board and knead for 10–15 minutes. Put the dough in a lightly oiled bowl, cover with clingfilm (or a cloth) and place in a warm dry place (such as an airing cupboard or a rack above a stove) for an hour.

Make the filling by putting the pecan nuts, sugar and cinnamon into a food-processor and whizzing until the ingredients are finely ground.

Once the dough has been rising for an hour, knead it for a further 5 minutes. Cut the dough into two and roll and stretch each piece on a lightly floured board until it measures about 25 x 35cm.

Brush some melted butter over the two pieces of dough. Sprinkle half the filling over each rectangle, then use a rolling pin to press it into the dough. Then, tightly roll each rectangle, starting at a long side, in order to create a Swiss-roll-like shape. Cut each log into 8 pieces (about 2cm thick) and put the swirls into 2 deep baking trays.

Make the topping by mixing together the pecan nuts, melted butter, sugar and syrup. Brush each side of the swirl slices with the mixture. Cover and place in a warm dry spot for a further 30 minutes. Make sure that you leave enough space between each of the swirls to allow them to rise and expand.

Preheat the oven to 190°C/gas mark 5. Once the swirls have risen, bake in the oven for 20 minutes. Leave to cool before eating (if you can!).

the lazy brunch

bloody mary

I adore having a Bloody Mary with brunch, especially after a late night out! Leave out the vodka to make a Virgin Mary.

makes 1

2 shots of vodka (about 2 capfuls)
juice of ½ lemon
5 dashes Worcestershire sauce
3 dashes Tabasco sauce
180ml tomato juice
pinch of sea salt and freshly ground
    black pepper
1 celery stick, to serve

Pour the vodka, lemon juice, Worcestershire sauce, Tabasco sauce and tomato juice into a glass, season with salt and pepper, and mix well with a spoon.

Serve with a stick of celery and 3 ice cubes in each glass.

---

cook's tip

brunch-time tipples

To make a Bellini, take 3 ripe peaches (peeled and pitted), pop them in a food-processor and purée. Divide the peach purée between 6 champagne flutes, top up with champagne or sparkling wine, and stir.

To make a Mimoso, take 500ml of fresh orange juice and chill. Just before serving, fill 6 champagne glasses with one-third orange juice and the rest of the glass with champagne or sparkling wine.

the relaxed sunday lunch

Sunday is the most perfect time to gather friends and family around for a little feast. Get everyone involved in the cooking and in laying the table. Food served in big dishes is the way to go so that no one feels stressed.

Sunday lunch is all about getting together at a relaxed, convivial table. A delicious roast, seasonal vegetables and a heavenly dessert are what the Sunday lunch table calls for. Once you have roasted your choice of meat, you can make the perfect gravy to accompany it by placing the roasting tin over a moderate heat to loosen the juices; this will take approximately 2-3 minutes. Scrape at the bits stuck to the base of the pan (they contain lots of delicious flavours), then pour in some stock, whisking as you do so. You can also add some red wine or cream at this stage, too. Strain the gravy through a sieve before you serve.

Everyone loves roast potatoes served with a roast. To make perfect roast potatoes, peel the potatoes, then parboil them for approximately 10 minutes. Drain the potatoes, toss in olive oil (or goose fat!), season with sea salt and freshly ground black pepper, and roast in a moderate oven for 30 minutes, giving them a toss every 5 minutes. For an Italian alternative, crush the roast potatoes when cooked and mix in some finely chopped black olives.

pine nut and rosemary crusted lamb

I love the crunchy crust on this lamb dish. You could also use thyme instead of the rosemary. I have often used this recipe for a leg of lamb and it works perfectly.

serves 4

50g pine nuts, roughly chopped
2 tablespoons roughly chopped fresh rosemary
1 garlic clove, crushed
50g butter, melted
4 x 2–3 cutlet racks of lamb, trimmed
sea salt and freshly ground black pepper

Preheat the oven to 180°C/gas mark 4.

Put the pine nuts, fresh rosemary and garlic in a bowl and pour over the melted butter. Mix and set aside.

Heat a frying pan and seal the racks of lamb on all sides. Place the racks of lamb in an ovenproof dish. Spread the pine nut and rosemary topping over the lamb.

Roast the lamb in the oven for 10–15 minutes for medium and a further 5–10 minutes for well done.

Take out of the oven, loosely cover with foil, and leave to rest for 10 minutes before serving.

roasting times

beef and lamb

240°C/gas mark 9 for 15 mins, then 200°C/gas mark 6

for rare
cook for 10 mins per 500g

for medium
cook for 14 mins per 500g

for well done
cook for 16–18 mins per 500g

chicken

220°C/gas mark 7 for 15 mins, then 190°C/gas mark 5

Cook for 20 mins per 500g

pork

220°C/gas mark 7 for 20 minutes then 180°C/gas mark 4

Cook for 20 mins per 500g

moroccan-spiced roast chicken

This spice mixture is also great for marinating a fillet of chicken breast for the barbecue or grilling in the kitchen. Simply add more olive oil so that it's more liquidy. I like to carve the chicken before I bring it to the table, and lay it all out on a large warmed platter that is bedded with some delicious spicy couscous.

serves 4

2 teaspoons ground cumin
1 teaspoon ground coriander
1 teaspoon mild chilli powder
1 teaspoon paprika
½ teaspoon ground cinnamon
2 garlic cloves, crushed
2 tablespoons lemon juice
2 tablespoons olive oil
1.5kg freerange or organic chicken
sea salt and freshly ground black pepper

Preheat the oven to 180°C/gas mark 4.

Put all the spices, garlic, lemon juice and olive oil in a bowl and mix well together.

Rinse the chicken under cold water and pat dry with kitchen paper.

Smear the spice mixture under the skin of the chicken, using a spoon or clean hands. This makes a world of difference to the final taste as the spices get right into the meat of the chicken.

Put the chicken in a roasting dish. Place the lemon halves that you juiced earlier into the cavity of the chicken. Season the chicken with salt and pepper and place in the oven for 70 minutes.

Baste the chicken by spooning the cooking juices from the bottom of the roasting dish over the chicken every 20 minutes.

To test if the chicken is cooked, pierce with a skewer (or a sharp knife). If the juices run clear, the chicken is cooked; if they are still pink, leave the chicken to cook for a further 10 minutes, and then test again.

Serve with my Moroccan-Spiced Couscous and Chickpea Salad (see page 42).

ways to roast a chicken

For all the following recipes, you will need 1 chicken (approx. 2.25kg in weight). Once prepared, put the chicken in a preheated oven at 180°C/gas mark 4 for 90 minutes.

paprika, garlic and lemon spiced chicken

to make: Put 1 garlic clove (crushed) in a bowl, whisk in the juice of 1 lemon, 80ml of olive oil and 1 dessertspoon of paprika, season with sea salt and freshly ground black pepper, and blend. Lift the flap of skin at the rear of the chicken and smear some of the spiced oil all over the meat under the skin. Rub the rest of the oil over the legs and wings.

serve with: Lemon and Thyme Roasties (page 87)

tarragon, white wine and garlic butter

to make: Place a saucepan over a low heat and pour in 1 tablespoon of olive oil. Stir in 2 shallots (finely diced) and 2 garlic cloves (crushed), and cook for 1 minute. Pour in 100ml of white wine and leave to cook for a further 3-4 minutes until the wine reduces. Take the pan off the heat and leave to cool. Place 60g of softened butter and 2 teaspoons of fresh tarragon in a bowl, add the shallots and garlic, and season with sea salt and freshly ground black pepper. Use the back of a spoon to blend everything together. Lift the flap of skin at the rear of the chicken and smear some of the butter all over the meat under the skin. Rub the rest of the butter over the legs and wings.

serve with: Celeriac and Potato Gratin (page 85)

indian-spiced roast chicken

to make: Whizz together 1 teaspoon of fresh ginger, 1 garlic clove, ½ teaspoon of ground coriander, 1 clove, a pinch of turmeric, 1 green chilli and 2 tablespoons of water until you have a thick paste. Mix 2 tablespoons of Greek yogurt and 2 teaspoons of lemon juice with the spice mix, season with sea salt and freshly ground black pepper, and blend. Lift the flap of skin at the rear of the chicken and smear some of the yogurt mix all over the meat under the skin. Rub the rest of the yogurt mix over the legs and wings.

serve with: Fresh Raita (page 176)

thai-style roast chicken

to make: Put 1 stick of lemongrass, 2 garlic cloves, ½ can of coconut milk, 2 teaspoons of fresh ginger, 2 tablespoons of fish sauce, 2 tablespoons of soy sauce, the juice of 1 lime and 2 sprigs of fresh coriander in a food-processor, season with salt and freshly ground black pepper, and blend. Lift the flap of skin at the rear of the chicken and smear some of the mix all over the meat under the skin. Rub the rest of the mix over the legs and wings.

serve with: Jasmine Rice

spiced apple loin of pork

The spicy apple flavours oozing their way into the loin of pork make for the most delicious roast pork, while the juices in the pan are sublime! After you have carved the pork loin, pour over the spicy apple juice from the pan. I particularly love this dish served with gratin Dauphinoise potatoes.

serves 4

50g butter
1 onion, diced
200g cooking apples, diced
100g brown sugar
4 cloves
1 teaspoon medium chilli powder
1 teaspoon turmeric powder
2.5cm piece of fresh ginger, peeled and finely chopped
100ml cider vinegar
2kg loin of pork
sea salt and freshly ground black pepper

Preheat the oven to 200°C/gas mark 6.

Melt the butter in a saucepan over a medium heat and add the apples and onions. Cook for 10 minutes, and then stir in the brown sugar, cloves, chilli powder, turmeric powder, fresh ginger and cider vinegar. Season with salt and pepper. Mix well.

Cover the saucepan and leave to simmer over a medium heat for 10 minutes. Take the lid off, turn down the heat and leave to cook for a further 5 minutes or until the apple has broken down and turned a rich golden brown colour.

Place the loin of pork in a large roasting tin and pour the spiced apple mixture all over the pork loin.

Roast in the oven for 1½ hours, basting the pork with the cooking juices from the bottom of the tin every 20 minutes.

roast rib of beef with creamy black pepper gravy

It's definitely worth making a trip to a good butcher to pick out a good rib of beef. The meat should be a dark brownish colour and not bright red. The darker colour means that it has been hung for longer and will therefore be more tender. Also, a thin marbling of fat all over the meat is something else to look out for because this means that the flavours from the fat will be dispersed throughout the meat.

serves 6

3kg rib of beef (on the bone)
bunch of fresh rosemary
2 garlic cloves, thinly sliced
1 teaspoon sea salt
1 teaspoon freshly ground
   black pepper
2 teaspoons olive oil

For the gravy
400ml single cream
1 teaspoon Dijon mustard
2 teaspoons freshly ground
   black pepper, plus a little extra
   for seasoning

Bring the rib of beef up to room temperature by taking it out of the fridge 30 minutes before cooking and leaving it to rest on the kitchen counter. This is important, as a cold piece of meat going into the oven will not be as tender.

Preheat the oven to 220°C/gas mark 7.

Using a knife, make 6 slits in the rib of beef and push a sprig of rosemary and a thin slice of garlic into the slits. Rub the sea salt and black pepper into the meat.

Place a roasting tin over a medium heat and add the olive oil. When the oil is hot, sear the meat on all sides until it is brown. Roast the beef in the oven for 20 minutes, then reduce the oven temperature to 160°C/gas mark 3 and continue to cook for 20 minutes per 450g of beef for medium or 15 minutes per 450g for rare.

When the beef is cooked, transfer to a serving dish, cover with tin foil and leave to rest for 30 minutes before carving. This will allow the meat to relax and tenderise.

Place the roasting tin over a warm hob and pour in the cream, mustard and black pepper. With a whisk gather all the delicious juices from the beef and mix in with the cream. The creamy gravy will begin to thicken after a couple of minutes.

Serve the gravy hot with the beef.

cook's tip

roast parsnips and carrots

Peel and cut 6 parsnips and 6 carrots into wedges. Place the vegetables in a roasting tin and put the meat that you are roasting on top. All the gorgeous juices from the meat will trickle down into the vegetables, making the best roast vegetables ever!

spring ratatouille

The great thing about making a large pan of ratatouille is that you can use some of it the following week, perhaps served with couscous, folded through pasta or in sandwiches with some goats' cheese.

serves 6

1 aubergine
1 courgette
1 red pepper, deseeded
1 yellow pepper, deseeded
1 garlic clove, crushed
400g tinned chopped tomatoes
olive oil
bunch of fresh basil
sea salt and freshly ground
  black pepper

Preheat the oven to 180°C/gas mark 4.

Slice the aubergine, courgette and peppers into wedges.

Put the vegetables, garlic and tomatoes in a roasting dish, season with salt and pepper, add a dollop of olive oil and mix well.

Bake in the oven for 30 minutes or until the vegetables are tender.

Stir in the fresh basil leaves just before serving.

celeriac and potato gratin

I love the aniseed flavour of celeriac. If you're not a huge fan of aniseed, just omit the celeriac and use all potato. You can also grate some Gruyère or Fontina cheese in between the layers.

serves 6

75g butter, softened,
    plus a little extra for greasing
1 garlic clove, crushed
900g potatoes, peeled and thinly sliced
500g celeriac, peeled, cut into quarters
    and thinly sliced
500ml creamy milk (half milk and half cream)
½ teaspoon freshly grated nutmeg
sea salt and freshly ground black pepper

Preheat the oven to 180°C/gas mark 4.

Grease a roasting dish with butter and sprinkle the crushed garlic on the bottom of the dish.

Drop the sliced potatoes and celeriac into a pan of boiling water for 4–5 minutes, then drain and make layers in the dish, overlapping the slices a little and seasoning each layer.

Pour the creamy milk over the potatoes and use your hand to push down the potatoes until they are completely immersed in the milk. Sprinkle the nutmeg over the potatoes and cover with tin foil.

Bake in the oven for 30 minutes. Remove the ton foil and turn up the heat to 200°C/gas mark 6 until the top is golden (about 20 minutes).

summer vegetable garden salad

This salad is so refreshing served with a roast. It's important that the vegetables are cut into thin cruditées. I would usually make this salad a couple of hours before lunch so that the oil, mustard and vinegar have a chance to infuse the vegetables.

serves 4

3 carrots
1 fennel bulb
1 cucumber
3 radishes
1 teaspoon Dijon mustard
6 tablespoons extra virgin olive oil
2 tablespoons white wine vinegar
70g toasted pine nuts
sea salt and freshly ground black pepper

Slice all the vegetables into thin cruditée sticks and place in a large serving bowl.

Whisk the mustard, olive oil and vinegar in a small bowl and season with salt and pepper.

Toss the vegetables in the dressing and sprinkle over the pine nuts.

spicy sweet potato fries

Sweet potatoes make such great chips, just be careful not to over cook them, as they can go very mushy. Delicious served with crème fraîche...

serves 6

1 teaspoon ground cumin
2 tablespoons olive oil
1kg sweet potatoes, peeled
sea salt and freshly ground black pepper

Preheat the oven to 200°C/gas mark 6.

In a small bowl, mix together the ground cumin and olive oil, season with salt and pepper and set aside.

Cut the sweet potatoes in half lengthways and cut each half into 6 wedges (fat chips!).

In a large bowl, mix together the potatoes and spiced oil mixture. Toss until the potatoes are evenly coated.

Arrange the potato fries in a roasting tray and roast in the oven for 35–40 minutes or until the edges are crisp and the potatoes are cooked through.

lemon and thyme roasties

The lemon juice in this dish adds a delicious zestiness to these roast potatoes. Rosemary is also a fabulous alternative to the thyme.

serves 6

700g potatoes (a floury variety
  such as King Edwards)
juice and skin of 1 lemon
100ml olive oil
4 sprigs of fresh thyme
2 garlic cloves
sea salt and freshly ground black pepper

Preheat the oven to 180°C/gas mark 4.

Wash and peel the potatoes. Chop the potatoes into small cubes and place in a pot of simmering salted water for 5 minutes, then drain and tip into a large bowl.

Pour the juice of the lemon and the olive oil onto the potatoes. Sprinkle the thyme into the bowl, add the garlic, season with salt and pepper, and mix well.

Chop up the lemon skins that you juiced and add to the potatoes for extra flavour.

Transfer the potatoes to a roasting dish and roast in the oven for 20 minutes, tossing them every 10 minutes so that they are thoroughly coated with all of the flavours.

Before serving, remove the lemon skins and whole garlic cloves.

italian rosemary crispbreads

I love to serve these crispbreads with salads. They are so simple to make and are fabulous stacked in the middle of the table for people to nibble on.

makes 8

125ml warm water
¼ teaspoon dried yeast
210g plain flour
2 tablespoons olive oil
1 egg
3 sprigs of fresh rosemary, finely chopped
sea salt

Preheat the oven to 180°C/gas mark 4.

Pour the water into a bowl and sprinkle in the dried yeast. Allow the yeast to foam, which should take about 5 minutes.

Put the flour in a large bowl, pour the yeast mixture on top, and add the olive oil and a sprinkle of sea salt. Stir together until a dough forms.

Tip the dough onto a floured surface and knead for 10 minutes. Transfer to an oiled bowl, cover with a tea-towel and place in a warm dry spot such as an airing cupboard for an hour.

Divide the dough into 8 pieces and roll each piece to roughly 24 x 10cm on a lightly floured surface.

Transfer to a baking sheet that has been lined with greaseproof paper. Brush with egg wash (using 1 egg and a splash of water whisked together), sprinkle with sea salt and fresh rosemary. Repeat with the remaining dough.

Bake in the oven for 20 minutes or until crisp and golden. Leave to cool on wire racks.

variation
Try adding some finely chopped black olives or sun-dried tomatoes to the recipe.

cook's tip

lovely gift ideas

These crispbreads also make a fabulous gift if you are visiting a friend's house for supper. Simply wrap them in greaseproof paper, tie with twine, and stick a sprig of rosemary in the knot.

baked cauliflower cheese

This is pure comfort food...
Sometimes, I use Gruyère
instead of the Cheddar
because it gives the dish a
more nutty flavour. It's also
a great dish to serve when
you have to feed lots of people
for lunch.

serves 4

1 small cauliflower
80g butter
80g plain flour
400ml milk
800g mature Cheddar cheese, grated
pinch of freshly ground black pepper

Preheat the oven to 180°C/gas mark 4.

Remove the outer leaves from the cauliflower and chop them coarsely.

Place the whole cauliflower and the chopped leaves in a saucepan with about 2.5cm of water. Cook on a medium heat for 10 minutes (you want the cauliflower florets to be slightly undercooked because they will be going in the oven too).

In a separate saucepan, make the cheese sauce by melting the butter and whisking in the flour. Cook for 2–3 minutes, stirring constantly. Add the milk gradually, whisking continuously to ensure that no lumps form. Stir in the grated cheese and pepper.

Place the cauliflower in a lightly buttered gratin dish and pour over the cheese sauce. Bake in the oven for 20 minutes and serve immediately.

creamed spinach with nutmeg

The great thing about this recipe is that it acts as both a sauce and a vegetable. It's delicious served with lamb, beef and chicken.

serves 4

50g butter
500g baby spinach
200ml single cream
pinch of freshly grated nutmeg
sea salt and freshly ground black pepper

Melt the butter in a large frying pan over a high heat, then pop in the baby spinach and cook for 2 minutes.

Pour the cream over the spinach and allow to cook for 5 minutes (you will see the cream thickening).

Scatter the nutmeg over and season with salt and pepper. Transfer to a warm serving bowl and serve.

variation
Try substituting the spinach with finely sliced mushrooms or purple-sprouting broccoli.

roasted artichokes with lemon thyme

This is absolutely delicious served on a piece of bruschetta (which is toasted sourdough with a drizzle of olive oil), mixed in a salad or just on its own for a starter with a lemon mayonnaise.

serves 2

6 artichoke hearts, boiled
juice of 1 lemon
olive oil
1 teaspoon finely chopped fresh thyme
sea salt and freshly ground black pepper

Preheat the oven to 180°C/gas mark 4.

Slice the cooked artichoke hearts into quarters and place on a baking tray. Drizzle over the lemon juice and some olive oil.

Sprinkle over the fresh thyme and season with salt and pepper. Mix well.

Bake in the oven for 10 minutes – and that's it!

---

cook's tip

preparing and cooking an artichoke

Firstly, snap off the stalk and cut off the pointed tips of the leaves with a pair of scissors. You can cook the artichoke in two ways. If you're cooking the artichoke whole, simmer in boiling water with the juice of one lemon for about 30 minutes, and then just pull away the leaves. If you simply want to use the heart, prise open the leaves from the top of the artichoke until you come to the hairy choke (heart). Tear the heart out and scoop away any fibres at the base with a teaspoon, and then you can either roast or boil the heart. The choke discolours very quickly, so keep it in a bowl of water with a few slices of lemon.

baked ricotta cake

This cake is fantastic because it lasts for 10 days and the flavour gets better as the days go by. Well, that's if it has a chance to...!

serves 10

400g ricotta
4 eggs, separated
2 tablespoons plain flour
grated zest and juice of 2 lemons
200g caster sugar
70g butter
12 digestive biscuits, crushed

Preheat the oven to 180°C/gas mark 4.

Place the ricotta in a bowl and mix in the yolks of the eggs, followed by the flour, lemon zest and juice, and caster sugar. Mix well.

In a separate bowl, whisk the egg whites until they are stiff and fold them into the ricotta mixture.

Place a saucepan over a low heat and melt the butter. Once the butter has melted, take the pan off the heat and stir in the crushed biscuits.

Spoon the biscuit mixture into a 24cm springform tin and press it down using the back of the spoon to create a biscuit base.

Pour the lemon ricotta mixture over the biscuit base. Bake in the oven for 55 minutes.

cook's tip

tempting alternatives

Once you have poured the cake mixture into the baking tin, cover with fresh blueberries, raspberries or white chocolate drops.

raspberry and rosewater roulade

I love flavouring meringues. You might like to try using orange-blossom or lavender water instead of the rosewater. It can even just be added to whipped cream for serving with cakes.

serves 6

For the meringue
5 egg whites
2 teaspoons rosewater
1 teaspoon white wine vinegar
1 teaspoon cornflour, sifted
225g caster sugar

For the filling
250ml double cream
2 teaspoons rosewater
1 tablespoon caster sugar
300g fresh raspberries

To decorate
fresh raspberries
icing sugar, for dusting

Preheat the oven to 130°C/gas mark ½.

To make the roulade, put the egg whites in a clean bowl and whisk with an electric whisk until soft peaks form. Fold in the rosewater, vinegar and cornflour.

Pour in the sugar bit by bit, continuing whisking until stiff peaks form.

Smooth the meringue in to a Swiss-roll tin, lined with tin foil, or smooth out into a circular shape to create a round pavlova. Bake in the oven for about 80–90 minutes until golden brown on the outside.

Turn off the oven, leaving the door slightly ajar, and leave the meringue to cool completely in the oven.

For the filling, lightly beat the cream and then beat in the rosewater and caster sugar.

Spread the rosewater cream evenly over the meringue and sprinkle the raspberries on top. Pull up the foil closest to you and roll the roulade away from you, starting with a short end.

Gently transfer the roulade to a serving dish using a cake slice. Dollop the remaining rosewater cream along the top, decorate with raspberries and lightly dust with icing sugar.

summer ice cream cake

This is a summer heavenly delight! If you wish, you can add chopped hazelnuts, almonds or grated chocolate to the mixture and you might also like to try raspberries or blueberries instead of the strawberries

serves 4

200ml whipping cream
6 large meringue nests
200g strawberries
2 teaspoons sugar

Whip the cream in a bowl and break up the meringue nests.

In a separate bowl, mash the strawberries and sugar together with a fork.

Fold the mashed strawberries into the whipped cream, followed by the crushed meringues.

Line a 450g loaf tin with clingfilm and tip in the strawberry and meringue mixture. Cover with more clingfilm and put in the freezer for 2–3 hours or until frozen.

Take the cake from the freezer just before serving. Remove the clingfilm from the top, turn the loaf tin over onto a plate or board, and then remove the rest of the clingfilm.

Slice the cake and serve.

the ultimate lemon tart!

The most important step when making this lemon tart is to chill the pastry so that you get a nice short (or crisp) result. You can make the tart the day before; in fact, I think it tastes better the next day.

serves 6

For the sweet shortcrust pastry
200g plain flour
1 tablespoon icing sugar
130g chilled butter, diced
1 egg yolk, beaten

For the filling
2 eggs, plus 2 egg yolks
grated zest and juice of 3 lemons
125g caster sugar
170ml double cream
icing sugar, for dusting

To make the pastry, sift together the flour and icing sugar, and then rub in the butter until the mixture resembles breadcrumbs. Stir in just enough egg yolk to bring the pastry together. Wrap the pastry in clingfilm and pop in the fridge for 30 minutes to chill.

Once the pastry has chilled, line a 23cm tart tin with the pastry and put in the fridge to chill for a further 20 minutes. (This will give a lovely, short, crisp finish to the pastry once it is baked.)

Preheat the oven to 190°C/gas mark 5.

Remove from the fridge, cover the pastry with baking parchment paper and fill with baking beans. Bake in the oven for 15 minutes.

While the pastry is baking, make the filling by placing the eggs and yolks, lemon zest, lemon juice and caster sugar in a large bowl and whisking. Slowly whisk in the cream.

Pour the lemon filling into the cooked pastry case. Reduce the heat of the oven to 180°C/gas mark 4 and bake the tart for 25–30 minutes or until the filling has set around the edges. The rest of the filling will set as it cools.

Remove the tart from the oven and leave to cool.

Once cooled, sift some icing sugar over the top of the tart.

variation
Try sprinkling 12 raspberries into the lemon filling and pushing them down with the back of a spoon before popping the tart in the oven.

apple pie sunday

I love serving this pie warm with a dollop of cinnamon whipped cream. Just whip together 200ml of cream with 1 dessertspoon of ground cinnamon – this is Sunday Heaven!

serves 6-8

For the pastry
280g plain flour
1 tablespoon sugar
1 teaspoon salt
250g chilled butter, diced
1 egg
1 tablespoon white wine vinegar
2 tablespoons water

For the filling
1kg cooking apples, peeled, cored, and diced
150g caster sugar
1 teaspoon ground cinnamon
1 tablespoon lemon juice
pinch of freshly grated nutmeg
1 teaspoon salt
2 tablespoons plain flour
1 egg, beaten

Firstly make the pastry by sieving the flour, sugar and salt into a large bowl. Rub the butter into the flour until it resembles breadcrumbs.

Mix together the egg and vinegar with the water and then mix into the breadcrumbs until the dough comes together. Divide the dough into 2 parts, wrap in clingfilm and chill in the fridge for an hour.

Preheat the oven to 180°C/gas mark 4.

Once the pastry is chilled, roll out the 2 pieces of dough on a lightly floured surface to a thickness of 5mm and line a 23cm pie pan with the dough.

Place the chopped apples, sugar, cinnamon, lemon juice, nutmeg, salt and flour in a bowl and toss well. Tip the filling into the pastry-lined dish and cover with the second sheet of pastry.

Crimp the edges with a fork and cut out a cross or heart shape in the middle. Brush with the beaten egg and bake in the oven for 50 minutes or until the pie is golden and cooked.

the decadent picnic

One of my best days last winter was taking a picnic and a ball down to the beach in Ireland with some friends. The food was great, we got to kick the ball around afterwards and it hardly cost us anything. You can't buy memories like that.

I love picnics, every part of them, including shopping at the market for breads and cheeses and buying little treats such as olives, artichokes and relishes at the deli. I love that everyone brings a dish along and am always astounded by the all-round scrumminess of friends' contributions. There is such a sense of anticipation as everyone lays out their delicious salads, quiches and tarts on the picnic rug. Afterwards, I lie back in the hazy sunshine and think, "This is it, this is heaven." But not quite, because just then someone reaches into the cool box and brings out the homemade cookies.

Not only are picnics a wonderfully enjoyable way to spend time outdoors, they are also such great value. Imagine how much the equivalent food would cost in a restaurant or how much it would cost to take the children out for a treat? With a picnic, you get the food, the family, the friends and the great outdoors. Picnics are about quality time. When you look back on your life, these are the days you'll remember.

what to pack

- Rug to sit on (plus some extra rugs to throw over your legs if it gets cold)
- Flask of hot water (for making tea)
- Cups, plates, glasses and cutlery
- Milk and sugar (kept in jam jars)
- Knife and board
- Cool box
- Napkins
- And a camera to capture the memory!

location

Picnics don't always have to take place on a cliff or a beach. You can take a picnic to a concert in the park, when walking by a lake or river, when visiting a nice wooded area, or even when going to a city park for the afternoon. Choose a combination of savoury and sweet picnic treats from the tantalizing recipes in this chapter.

Enjoy your picnic!

fabulous sandwich fillers

Here are a few ideas for delicious sandwich fillers. You might also like to try the other ideas for fillings in The Envied Lunchbox, on pages 36–37.

cheesy apple slaw
Mix grated hard cheese with grated apple, chopped spring onions, a squeeze of lemon juice and a little mayonnaise. Delicious with wholemeal bread or rolls.

salmon and cream cheese bagels
Cut the smoked salmon into bite-sized pieces, mix with diced cucumber, cream cheese and a squeeze of lemon. Delicious spread over bagels.

creamy smoked mackerel
Skin and flake some smoked mackerel fillets, then mix with a little mayonnaise and Greek yogurt. Spread onto thick wholemeal bread and top with crisp lettuce leaves.

italian roasted vegetable
Roast 1 sliced courgette, aubergine and red pepper with some olive oil. Once roasted, mix with a little sour cream, lemon juice and fresh basil. Delicious on a baguette. You could also add in some feta or soft goats' cheese.

old-fashioned egg salad

This is delicious, but I also love mixing in some diced cucumber and tomatoes, and then sandwiching the egg salad between 2 slices of white sourdough bread.

serves 4

8 hard-boiled eggs
2 spring onions, finely sliced
1 teaspoon Dijon mustard
4 tablespoons mayonnaise
sea salt and freshly ground black pepper

Dice the 8 hard-boiled eggs and place in a large bowl.

Tip in the spring onions, mustard and mayonnaise. Season with salt and pepper, and mix well.

variation
You can also add 1 tablespoon of capers or gherkins or, alternatively, 70g of cooked smoked bacon lardons to make the egg salad even more delicious.

winter coleslaw

Try adding some finely chopped hazelnuts to this recipe for an extra nutty flavour and crunch. It will last for about 1 week in the fridge and it always tastes better the day after it has been made. (pictured opposite).

serves 6

80-100g Greek yogurt
1 teaspoon Dijon mustard
finely grated zest of 1 lemon
juice of ½ lemon
small red cabbage, finely sliced
2 carrots, grated
½ celeriac, grated
1 tablespoon chopped celeriac leaves (celery or flat-leaf parsley leaves may also be used)
sea salt and freshly ground black pepper

Put the yogurt, mustard, lemon zest and juice in a small bowl, and mix well.

Tip all of the vegetables into a large bowl, pour over the liquid, and mix well.

Season with salt and pepper, give the coleslaw one last toss, and it is ready to be eaten!

spring coleslaw

Making spring coleslaw is so simple, and the difference in taste to the shop-bought version is vast, so it is well worth making it homemade!

serves 6

4 tablespoons plain yogurt
4 tablespoons mayonnaise
1 tablespoon lemon juice
½ teaspoon Dijon mustard
½ head of white cabbage, very thinly sliced
2 spring onions, very thinly sliced
2 carrots, coarsely grated
sea salt and freshly ground black pepper

Mix together the yogurt, mayonnaise, lemon juice and mustard.

Put all the vegetables into a large bowl and pour over the dressing. Season and mix very well.

The coleslaw will keep for 3 days in a fridge.

café de flore's quiche lorraine

Café de Flore is one of my favourite cafés in Paris and the quiche is one of my favourite dishes on the menu. Sunday brunch is always the best time to go there. This is my variation of their famous quiche.

serves 6-8

For the pastry
175g plain flour, plus extra
   for dusting
pinch of salt
75g chilled butter, diced,
   plus extra for greasing
1 egg

For the filling
150g Cheddar, grated
200g smoked bacon lardons
5 eggs, beaten
100ml milk
200ml single cream
4 tomatoes, sliced (optional)
2 sprigs of fresh thyme
sea salt and freshly ground
   black pepper

To make the pastry, sift the flour and salt into a large bowl. Rub in the butter until you have a soft breadcrumb texture. Add the whisked egg to bring the crumb mixture together to form a firm dough (if needed you can add a little cold water too). Wrap the pastry in clingfilm and rest in the fridge for 30 minutes.

Roll out the pastry on a lightly floured surface and line a well-buttered 22cm flan dish. Don't cut off the edges of the pastry yet. Chill again.

Preheat the oven to 190°C/gas mark 5.

Remove the pastry case from the fridge, line the base with baking parchment and then fill with baking beans. Place on a baking tray and bake blind for 20 minutes. Remove the beans and parchment, and return the pastry base to the oven for a further 5 minutes. Reduce the temperature of the oven to 160°C/gas mark 3.

Sprinkle the grated cheese over the pastry base.

Fry the bacon pieces until they are crisp then sprinkle them over the top of the cheese.

Combine the eggs with the milk and cream in a bowl, and season well. Pour the mixture over the bacon and cheese. Add the sliced tomatoes (if using), sprinkle the thyme over the top, and trim the edges of the pastry.

Bake for 30–40 minutes or until set. Remove from the oven and leave to cool and set further.

Serve in wedges.

pesto ricotta tart

I learned this recipe in Italy. Buy some ready-to-roll filo pastry, and this recipe will be a cinch to make! It's a fabulous dish to serve when going for a picnic, but also great for lunch or as a starter served with a green salad.

serves 4

50g butter, plus extra for greasing
1 large leek, trimmed and thinly sliced
2 large eggs
4 tablespoons single cream
150g ricotta
100g freshly grated Parmesan cheese
3 tablespoons chunky basil pesto (see page 208 for my Summer Basil Pesto recipe)
2 tablespoons finely chopped fresh parsley leaves
8 sheets of filo pastry
sea salt and freshly ground black pepper

Preheat the oven to 180°C/gas mark 4.

Lightly butter a 23cm pie plate and set aside. Heat 15g of the butter in a frying pan over a medium heat. Tip in the leek and cook, stirring often, until soft. Transfer the leek to a large bowl and set aside to cool.

Whisk the eggs in a medium-sized bowl. Add to the leeks along with the ricotta, Parmesan cheese, pesto, parsley, and salt and pepper. Stir to combine and set aside.

Melt the remaining butter. Lay one sheet of filo in the prepared pie plate. Brush the filo with the melted butter, leaving the outer 4cm rim unbrushed. Repeat with 7 more sheets of filo.

Trim the edges to match the shape of the pie plate and pour in the filling. Brush the top of the filo rim with butter, and bake in the oven for about 40 minutes or until the edges are golden brown and the filling has set. Cool before serving.

summer savoury tart

In the autumn, I substitute the tomatoes and courgettes for diced roasted butternut squash or smoked bacon lardons for a seasonal change.

serves 6-8

250g ready-made shortcrust pastry
1 tablespoon olive oil
2 courgettes, sliced
270g cooked new potatoes, sliced
400g tomatoes, sliced
100g grated Gruyère
handful of basil leaves
3 eggs
200ml crème fraîche
150ml milk
50g freshly grated Parmesan cheese
sea salt and freshly ground black pepper

Preheat the oven to 200°C/gas mark 6.

Roll out the pastry to a 30cm round and line a deepish, loose-based 20–22.5cm tart tin. Line the pastry case with greaseproof paper and fill with baking beans. Bake in the oven for 15 minutes, then remove the paper and beans and bake for a further 5 minutes until the pastry is pale golden. Reduce the temperature to 180°C/gas mark 4.

Place a frying or griddle pan over a medium heat, add the olive oil and fry the courgettes until they are lightly browned on each side.

Layer half the potatoes, courgettes and tomatoes in the pastry case, season between layers, and sprinkle over a little Gruyère and a few basil leaves. Repeat, finishing with a layer of tomatoes.

Beat together the eggs, crème fraîche and milk. Season, then stir in the remaining Gruyère and two-thirds of the Parmesan cheese.

Pour this mixture over the filling and sprinkle with the rest of the Parmesan cheese.

Bake in the oven for 35–45 minutes until golden and firm to the touch. Scatter with the remaining basil leaves. Leave to cool for 10 minutes or so before serving.

lemon and rocket salad

This is delicious served with my Café de Flore's Quiche Lorraine on page 106.

serves 4

200g crème fraîche
grated zest and juice of 1 lemon
1 tablespoon Dijon mustard
800g new potatoes, cooked
bunch of fresh rocket
sea salt and freshly ground black pepper

Mix together the crème fraîche, lemon juice and zest, and mustard in a bowl.

Slice the potatoes in half. While they are still warm, mix in the dressing. Season with salt and pepper. Fold in the fresh rocket. Stir gently and leave to cool.

easy italian pasta salad

Try substituting the mozzarella with a fresh goats' cheese or ricotta. You can also serve this hearty pasta salad warm.

serves 4

400g dried fusilli pasta
1 red pepper, deseeded
8 cherry tomatoes, halved
12 black olives, halved
200g mozzarella cheese, cut into
   bite-sized pieces
bunch of fresh basil leaves, torn
extra virgin olive oil, for drizzling
sea salt and freshly ground
   black pepper

Preheat the oven to 180°C/gas mark 4.

Bring a large pan of salted water to the boil and cook the fusilli until it is al dente. Drain the pasta and run it under cold water.

Roast the red pepper for 20 minutes.

Transfer the roasted pepper to a bowl, cover with clingfilm and leave for 10 minutes as this allows the steam to loosen the skin of the pepper.

Remove from the bowl, peel off the skin and dice the flesh.

Transfer the pasta to a large bowl and mix in the roasted pepper, tomatoes, olives, mozzarella and basil.

Drizzle with a good dollop of extra virgin olive oil and season with salt and pepper.

spanish tortilla

I love adding sliced chorizo or red peppers to this tortilla. It's also absolutely delicious served with a drizzle of fresh homemade Summer Basil Pesto on top (see page 208).

serves 8

10 freerange or organic eggs
2 tablespoons olive oil
3 onions, thinly sliced
600g potatoes, peeled and diced
sea salt and freshly ground black pepper

In a bowl, lightly whisk the eggs. Place a 20cm frying pan over a medium heat and pour in half the olive oil. When the oil is hot, tip in the onions and potatoes, then reduce the heat and leave them to cook for 15 minutes, making sure that you come back to the pan every few minutes to stir.

Once the potatoes and onions are cooked, put them in the bowl of whisked eggs, season with salt and pepper, and mix together.

Place the frying pan back over a low heat, add the remaining olive oil, and pour in the egg, potato and onion mixture. Leave to cook for about 15 minutes or until the egg mixture has set.

Flipping the tortilla over can be a bit tricky, so bear with me! Place a plate over the pan and flip the pan over so that the tortilla comes out onto the plate, cooked side up. Slide the tortilla back into the pan with the cooked side facing upwards. Leave to cook for a further 5 minutes.

Once cooked, you can eat the tortilla either hot or cold. Delicious with a big green salad.

my farmers' market pâté

Years ago I had stalls at various farmers' markets in southern Ireland. This pâté it still the bestseller today in my restaurants! It will keep for 1 week in the fridge.

serves 10

For the pâté
450g butter, softened
675g chicken livers, cleaned
2 tablespoons brandy
1 garlic clove, crushed
2 teaspoons fresh thyme

For the caramelised onions
20g butter
2 onions, sliced
1 tablespoon brown mustard seeds

Melt a knob of the butter in a frying pan and add the chicken livers. Cook over a medium heat for about 15 minutes, stirring occasionally. When the chicken livers are cooked, there should be no trace of redness in the meat. Transfer the cooked livers to a food-processor.

Add the brandy, garlic and thyme to the frying pan and deglaze by scraping up all the tiny pieces of meat and juices from the livers using a whisk – the bottom of the pan is where the real flavour is! Add the brandy mixture to the food-processor and blend with the livers. Leave to cool.

While the livers are cooling, make the caramelised onions. Melt the butter in a saucepan and stir in the onions. Reduce the heat, cover the pan and leave to sweat for about 5 minutes.

Remove the lid, turn up the heat and stir in the mustard seeds. Continue cooking until the onions have softened and become a rich brown colour. Leave to cool.

Slowly add the remaining butter to the cooled chicken liver mixture and mix until all the butter has blended. Fold in the caramelised onions.

Transfer the mixture to a large dish, cover and leave to set in the fridge for at least 3 hours.

If you want to preserve the pâté for longer, pour some clarified butter on top before setting in the fridge. This way it will keep for up to 2 weeks.

This pâté is delicious served with some hot crunchy white bread.

variation
To make Smoked Bacon and Rosemary Pâté, omit the caramelised onions, thyme and mustard seeds, and add 100g of smoked bacon lardons when cooking the livers. Replace the thyme with fresh rosemary.

chocolate and almond cake

Now who doesn't love chocolate cake...? This mouthwatering chocolate cake is as intense as it is delicious. I always use Valrhona chocolate when I am making it.

serves 10

150g good-quality dark chocolate (minimum 70% cocoa solids), broken into pieces
150g butter
4 eggs, separated
90g caster sugar
80g self-raising flour
150g ground almonds
flaked almonds for the topping

For the chocolate icing
150g good-quality dark chocolate (minimum 70% cocoa solids), broken into pieces
150g unsalted butter, diced

Preheat the oven to 180°C/gas mark 4.

Place the chocolate and butter in a bowl over a pan of gently simmering water. Leave until melted and smooth, stirring every few minutes. Leave to cool.

Put the egg yolks and caster sugar in a separate bowl and whisk until thick and creamy. Fold in the cooled chocolate mixture, followed by the flour and then the ground almonds. Mix well.

In another bowl, whisk the egg whites until they form soft peaks. Gently fold into the chocolate mixture until completely combined.

Pour the mixture into a lined 24cm spring-form cake tin and bake in the oven for 45–50 minutes or until just firm to the touch. Remove from the oven and leave to cool in the tin.

To make the chocolate icing, place the chocolate in a heatproof bowl over a pan of simmering water and whisk in the butter until it has melted. Remove the bowl from the heat and whisk every few minutes while the icing is cooling.

Once the cake and icing have cooled, ice the cake with the chocolate icing, and sprinkle some flaked almonds on top to decorate.

homemade jammie dodgers

I loved Jammie Dodgers as a child and I guess this is really my more adult version of the well-loved biscuit!

makes 12-16

250g unsalted butter, softened
350g plain flour
125g icing sugar,
   plus extra for sprinkling
pinch of sea salt
200g strawberry or raspberry jam

Preheat the oven to 180°C/gas mark 4.

Beat the butter until it is light and fluffy. Add the flour, icing sugar and salt. Combine all the ingredients until you have a nice dough. Wrap the dough ball in clingfilm and chill in the fridge for 1 hour.

After chilling, roll out the dough and cut into rounds with a circular-shaped cookie cutter. Place half of the biscuits on a baking tray lined with parchment paper.

For the other half of the biscuits, cut out a heart shape in the middle and place on a second lined baking tray.

Bake both sets of biscuits in the oven for 6–8 minutes. Leave to cool.

Spread half of the biscuits with jam and cover with the heart-shaped biscuits.

Sprinkle icing sugar on top.

homemade lemon and lime cordial

Make a big batch of the cordial because it will last for approximately 3 months in a sterilised bottle and it's always so handy to have in the fridge.

makes 1 litre

1 tablespoon grated lemon rind
2 teaspoons grated lime rind
200ml lemon juice
200ml lime juice
265g caster sugar
600ml boiling water

Place the lemon and lime rind, lemon and lime juice, and sugar in a saucepan. Add the boiling water and stir until the sugar has dissolved. Leave to cool.

Pour the cordial into a sterilised bottle.

To serve, use one-third of a cup of cordial to two-thirds of a cup of chilled sparkling mineral water or iced water. Serve with thinly sliced lemon and lime and a sprig of mint.

the heavenly afternoon tea

I'm a huge fan of afternoon tea - and I don't mean a tea bag in a mug with a biscuit. I'm talking about five different kinds of beautiful little finger sandwiches, a tea bread with melted butter, fresh buttermilk scones and wonderful homemade cakes.

Afternoon tea needn't be something traditional and expensive in a grand hotel. You can pull it off with great aplomb at home for very little cost. It's also a wonderful excuse to dust off that china you've been saving for best and get out your prettiest cloths and napkins. If you don't have a set of china, treat yourself - you can buy sets of beautiful china cheaply in charity shops. The tea has to be perfectly brewed using loose tea and served in china cups and saucers. Trust me, tea really does taste better out of a china cup and it looks so much prettier.

Inviting friends round for afternoon tea is a relaxed and fun thing to do; it also feels a little bit decadent. I enjoy the preparation, too; baking is such a pleasurable way to spend a few hours and I feel so proud when I see my sumptuous cakes and tea breads cooling on the trays. Serving afternoon tea for a friend's birthday or pre-wedding bash can also be a really relaxed alternative to a more formal occasion. You can add a touch of glamour with delicate little cupcakes and delicious macaroons or try my Semolina Cake with Honey and Pistachio. Afternoon tea is a pretty, sweet, buttery affair, but if your friends are anything like mine, they'll love it.

how to make the perfect pot of tea

Fill the tea pot with water from the hot tap to warm it prior to adding tea leaves and boiling water.

Fill the kettle with fresh, cold, non-distilled water.

Just before the kettle begins to boil, pour the warm water from the tea pot and add one teaspoon of tea leaves per cup, plus an additional teaspoon 'for the pot'.

Remove the kettle from the heat right after it comes to the boil, and pour 250ml per cup into the tea pot.

Let the tea steep for 3–7 minutes, depending on desired strength.

Add cold whole milk or lemon to the tea cups, according to the preference of your guests.

Pour the tea into the cups, using a tea strainer to catch loose leaves.

finger sandwiches

There is something so decadent about de-crusted finger sandwiches. An afternoon tea is just not right without them! Here are a couple of recipes for egg salad and cucumber and smoked salmon finger sandwiches. Home-cooked ham with mustard and Cheddar cheese is another classic. Both recipes below make 8 finger sandwiches.

egg salad

This is a really comforting filling for an afternoon-tea sandwich.

3 eggs
1 tablespoon crème fraîche
2 teaspoons finely chopped fresh flat-leaf parsley
4 slices of good-quality sliced white bread
sea salt and freshly ground black pepper

Boil the eggs for 8 minutes. Drain and leave to cool.

Peel the eggs and mash them with the crème fraîche and parsley, and season with salt and pepper. Mix well.

Spread the egg salad on 2 slices of bread and put the remaining slices of bread on top. Cut off the crusts and slice each sandwich into 4 finger sandwiches, making 8 finger sandwiches in total.

cucumber and smoked salmon

A classic combination, this sandwich filling always feels slightly decadent. Be sure to use the best-quality smoked salmon you can find.

1 tablespoon mayonnaise
2 teaspoons fresh dill
4 slices of oak-smoked salmon
10 thin slices of cucumber
4 slices of good-quality sliced brown bread
sea salt and freshly ground black pepper

Put the mayonnaise and dill in a bowl, and mix well.

Spread the dill mayonnaise on 2 slices of bread and put the salmon slices and cucumber on top. Season to taste.

Place the remaining slices of bread on top. Cut off the crusts and slice each sandwich into 4 finger sandwiches, making 8 finger sandwiches in total.

short scones

These short scones are half way between a plain scone and a shortcake biscuit. They taste divine served with clotted cream and homemade jam (see my recipe for Summer Fruit Jam on page 20).

makes 8

300g plain flour,
  plus extra for dusting
50g caster sugar
1 tablespoon baking powder
130g butter
1 egg, beaten, plus a little extra
  for brushing
100ml single cream

Sift the flour, sugar and baking powder into a large bowl.

Grate the butter into the flour and mix together until the mixture resembles breadcrumbs.

In a separate bowl, beat together the egg and cream. Pour into the flour mixture, and bring the liquid and flour together until they form a dough.

Dust both hands with flour and transfer the dough from the bowl to a floured working surface. Roll out the dough until it is about 2cm thick and cut out 8 rounds with a pastry cutter.

Brush lightly with some beaten egg and put in the fridge for 1 hour to chill.

Preheat the oven to 220°C/gas mark 7.

Bake in the oven for 10 minutes or until the scones are lightly golden brown.

madeleines

Madeleines are deliciously light and so simple to make. The only tricky thing is that you do need a madeleine tin to make these, as it gives the cakes their distinctive shape.

makes 24

200g plain flour, plus extra for dusting
1 teaspoon baking powder
140g caster sugar
4 eggs
200g unsalted butter, softened,
   plus a little extra for greasing
2 teaspoons vanilla extract
2 tablespoons icing sugar

Preheat the oven to 180°C/gas mark 4.

Sift the flour and baking powder into a large bowl.

In a separate bowl, whisk together the sugar and eggs with an electric whisk until they are fluffy, followed by the butter.

Using a spatula, fold in the flour mixture and vanilla extract. Cover the bowl and put in the fridge for 20 minutes to chill.

Grease a 24-hole madeleine tin with butter and dust with flour. Using a spoon, fill each mould with the mixture.

Bake in the oven for 10 minutes or until golden in colour.

Leave to cool in the tin for 5 minutes and then tip onto a cooling rack.

Dust with the icing sugar.

semolina cake with honey and pistachio

Yes, it tastes as good as it looks! Sweet, sticky, and with a little crunch, it is one of the most heavenly cakes that I have made.

makes 1 cake

4 large eggs
150g caster sugar
125ml vegetable oil
110g plain flour
110g semolina
1½ teaspoons baking powder
pinch of salt
175g pistachios, finely ground
1 teaspoon grated lemon zest
2 tablespoons pistachios, chopped

For the syrup
300g honey
250ml water
1 tablespoon lemon juice

Preheat the oven to 180°C/gas mark 4.

Place the eggs and sugar in a large bowl, and beat together with an electric mixer on high speed for about 5 minutes. Reduce the speed and slowly pour in the vegetable oil.

Tip in the flour, semolina, baking powder and salt, and mix well until the mixture comes together.

Fold in the ground pistachios and lemon zest.

Pour the cake mixture into a greased 24cm spring-form tin and bake in the oven for 30–35 minutes.

Meanwhile, make the syrup by stirring the honey, water and lemon juice in a saucepan and placing over a high heat. Leave the syrup to boil and reduce by half, which takes about 10 minutes.

Use a skewer to poke deep holes in the cake while it is still hot. Drizzle half of the syrup evenly over the top, allowing it to be absorbed, then pour over the remaining syrup. Leave to cool completely, then sprinkle with the chopped pistachios.

Serve with a dollop of mascarpone cream.

old-fashioned victoria sponge

Every Saturday when I was a child we would have a Victoria sponge cake. It's such a simple recipe – just a light sponge with strawberries and cream – but sometimes the simplest things are the best. When fresh strawberries aren't in season, use strawberry jam instead.

makes 1 cake

220g butter, plus extra for greasing
220g caster sugar
4 eggs
220g self-raising flour
pinch of salt
2 tablespoons warm water
200ml whipped cream
300g strawberries, hulled and sliced
icing sugar, for dusting

Preheat the oven to 190°C/gas mark 5.

Grease and line three 18cm sandwich tins with greaseproof paper.

In a large bowl, cream together the butter and sugar using a wooden spoon or an electric mixer. Beat in the eggs one at a time.

Sift the flour and salt into the bowl, add the warm water, and mix well.

Transfer to the prepared tins and bake in the oven for 15–20 minutes. Let cool.

Place one of the sponges on a cake stand and spread over half of the whipped cream followed by half of the sliced strawberries. Place another sponge on top and repeat, finishing with the third sponge on the top.

Dust with icing sugar.

irish tea brack

This traditional Irish tea brack is a great way of using up all those dried fruits that get leftover after the Christmas baking. The brack will last for up to 2 weeks.

makes 1 loaf

350g mixed dried fruit (raisins, sultanas and currants)
300ml cold tea
120g caster sugar
1 egg, beaten
250g plain flour
2 teaspoons baking powder
2 teaspoons mixed spice

Place the dried fruit in a bowl and cover with the cold tea. Leave to soak overnight.

Next day, place the sugar and egg in a bowl. Sift in the flour, baking powder and mixed spice and mix all the ingredients together.

Preheat the oven to 180°C/gas mark 4.

Pour the soaked fruits and any remaining tea into the bowl and mix together well.

Tip into a greased 1kg loaf tin and bake in the oven for 1 hour.

Allow to cool on a wire tray.

homemade feta and sun-dried tomato sausages

Children love making these sausages, as they are such fun to make. There are lots of variations that you can try, including sage and grated apple; garlic and thyme; or cajun-spiced. I love eating my sausages with wet polenta or creamy whipped potatoes.

serves 5

8 semi sun-dried tomatoes, finely chopped
450g minced free-range pork
 (from the neck or shoulder)
80g feta cheese
1 tablespoon dried oregano
1 egg, beaten
plain flour, for dusting
olive oil, for frying
sea salt and freshly ground black pepper

Put the sun-dried tomatoes in a mixing bowl with the minced pork, feta cheese, dried oregano and beaten egg. Season with salt and pepper, and mix well.

Divide the mixture into 10 pieces and roll each one into a sausage shape.

Sprinkle a thin layer of plain flour on a baking tray and roll the sausages in the flour. Rock the sausages back and forth in your hands to remove any excess flour. You want the sausages to be very lightly coated in the flour.

Put the sausages on a clean tray and leave to chill in a fridge for 1 hour (this will help the sausages to hold their shape).

Place a frying pan over a medium heat and add a dollop of olive oil. Add the sausages one by one and gently cook for about 10 minutes, turning every couple of minutes to make sure that they are evenly cooked.

Serve with creamy mashed potatoes or wet polenta (see Cook's Tip, left).

cook's tip

making wet polenta

Pour 1 litre of water into a large saucepan, add 1 tablespoon of sea salt and place over a high heat. When the water has come to the boil, whisk in 400g of polenta and turn the heat down to the lowest possible setting. With a wooden spoon, keep stirring the polenta every few minutes – it takes about 10-15 minutes to cook. Then, season with freshly ground black pepper and mix in a good slurp of olive oil.

orange rice pudding with raspberry jam

This was my favourite dessert as a child and I still get cravings for it. It's so cheap to make and a great stand-by dessert as well. I love to cook these rice puddings in little individual ceramic pots to serve at a dinner party and pop a nice big Kilner jar of jam in the centre of the table so that everyone can just help themselves.

serves 2

30g butter
80g short-grain rice
grated zest and juice of 1 orange
55g caster sugar
50g sultanas
1 teaspoon freshly grated nutmeg
900ml milk
jar of homemade raspberry jam

Preheat the oven to 160°C/gas mark 3.

Grease a 1.2-litre pie dish with 10g of the butter.

Put the rice, orange zest, sugar, sultanas and nutmeg in a bowl, and mix well. Pour the rice mixture into the prepared pie dish.

Pour the milk and orange juice over the rice. Slice the remaining 20g of butter and place on top.

Bake in the oven for 1½ hours, stirring a couple of times.

Serve with the homemade raspberry jam.

variation
You can make a Rosewater Rice Pudding by omitting the orange juice and zest and adding 2 tablespoons of rosewater. This is delicious served with fresh raspberries.

apple and blackberry crumble with vanilla custard

Now who doesn't love a warm fruity crumble served with a big dollop of cream? Try adding 1 tablespoon of brown sugar to the crumble topping to get an extra sweet and crunchy top.

serves 6

For the filling
500g cooking apples
80g sugar
1 tablespoon water
200g blackberries

For the crumble
80g chilled butter, diced
150g plain flour
50g brown sugar
50g hazelnuts, chopped

For the custard
600ml milk
1 vanilla pod, slit
3 egg yolks
25g caster sugar
1 teaspoon cornflour

Preheat the oven to 200°C/gas mark 6.

To make the filling, put the apples, sugar and water into a saucepan and simmer until the apples are beginning to break down (you don't want to end up with a mush because the apples are going to be cooked further in the oven). Remove from the heat, stir in the blackberries, and leave to cool.

Meanwhile, make the crumble by rubbing the butter into the flour. Add the sugar and chopped hazelnuts.

Put the filling in an ovenproof pie dish or into individual ramekin dishes, and sprinkle the crumble on top. Bake in the oven for 45 minutes if you are using a pie dish and 25 minutes if you are using individual ramekins, or until the crumble is golden in colour.

While the crumble is cooking, make the custard by heating the milk with the vanilla pod over a medium heat until it comes to a simmer, then remove from the heat.

Mix together the egg yolks, sugar and cornflour until you get a smooth paste.

Place the milk back over the heat and stir in the egg mixture. Reduce the heat to low and continue to stir the custard until it thickens.

Remove the vanilla pod (rinse it under water and dry it so that you can use it again).

cook's tip

using old vanilla pods

You can make vanilla sugar by placing used vanilla pods in the centre of a large jar of caster sugar and giving the jar a good shake to make sure the vanilla is buried. Within a week the caster sugar will be scented with vanilla. Great for baking!

banana bread pudding

I also love making this pudding with brioche and sprinkling chocolate drops through the layers for a really decadent bread pudding. Delicious served with the Vanilla Custard on the opposite page.

serves 6

25g butter, plus extra for greasing
10 thin slices of bread
2 bananas, sliced
2 teaspoons ground cinnamon
300ml milk
100ml single cream
2 freerange or organic eggs
25g brown sugar
pinch of freshly grated nutmeg

Preheat the oven to 190°C/gas mark 5.

Grease a 1.2-litre pie dish with 10g of the butter.

Spread each slice of bread on one side with butter and cut into triangles.

Arrange a layer of bread, buttered-side up, in the bottom of the dish, then add a layer of banana. Sprinkle with a little cinnamon, then repeat the layers of bread, banana and cinnamon until you have used up all of the bread. Finish with a layer of bread, and set aside.

Gently warm the milk and cream in a saucepan over a low heat.

Crack the eggs into a bowl, add the sugar, and whisk lightly.

Add the warm milk and cream mixture to the whisked eggs, and stir well.

Pour over the prepared bread layers and push the bread down using a wooden spoon to make sure that it is completely covered in the liquid.

Sprinkle with nutmeg and leave to stand for 30 minutes.

Bake in the oven for 30–40 minutes or until the custard has set and the top is a golden brown colour.

Making a selection of dips yourself will make your guests feel really special.

Homemade Vanilla Fudge, Hot Chocolate Mix or Cookie Dough are lovely gifts for your guests to take home.

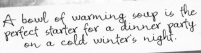

A bowl of warming soup is the perfect starter for a dinner party on a cold winter's night.

the divine dinner party

homemade table settings

apéritifs

simple dinner party menus

homemade edible gifts

homemade table settings

When I think about the most memorable meals I've eaten, I also remember the location and the table setting. The table setting gives a first impression and sets the tone, creating a sense of occasion, atmosphere and mood. I have three golden rules. First, keep it seasonal, following the flowers, fauna, colours and mood of the time of year; second, bear in mind that you want your guests to enjoy themselves; and third, keep it simple by avoiding conflicting patterns in the tablecloth and napkins and by using the same type or colour of flowers. And, for heaven's sake, avoid overhead lights and instead use candles or little lamps to give a soft flattering light. Try to match the accessories to the occasion, whether this is festive, glamorous, romantic or magical. At Christmas, for example, what could be easier than taking a piece of ribbon and tying a name card to the back of each guest's chair with a sprig of holly and fir? Or, for spring, pick a handful of wild flowers, such as daisies, and tie three on each napkin with a yellow ribbon. It is so simple, yet will really delight your guests. And that's the thing, it's not about expense, but about using what's readily to hand, as well as personal flair to surprise, inspire or amuse them.

alfresco dining

this page The most elegant tables are often the simplest. Daisies look so beautiful tied with a piece of ribbon and placed on your guests' napkins. You could also tie a flower to the backs of the chairs. Fresh flowers look wonderful, but a few sprigs of dried lavender also look great.

mid-summer night supper

above and left Seasonal flowers are always the most beautiful and a single flower on each plate makes such a statement. Use old vases, perhaps made from pewter, to give the table a natural look.

below Match the colours of the accessories on the table. Here, the mustard-coloured velvet ribbons that I used to tie the napkins work beautifully with the lavender colour of the irises.

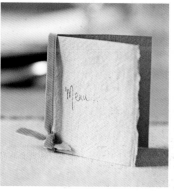

christmas party

above left and top right Wrap ivy leaves around a piece of wire to create a natural-looking wreath. Put a candle in a glass night-light holder and hang it from the wreath with ribbon.

above right Make a menu card for each guest. They are simple to make and some red velvet ribbon adds a festive touch.

far left A sprig of pine and laurel, velvet ribbon and a name card attached to the back of each chair look so pretty.

left Wrap some pretty ribbon around plain candlestick holders.

inexpensive decorating tips

Here are just a few simple, but effective, suggestions for making your dinner-party setting look beautiful:

Type up the menu that you will be serving and print it out on some sea-blue paper. Then, place the menus on peoples' plates with a sea-shell or pine cone holding them down.

Buy a roll of brightly coloured ribbon and cut it into 15cm strips. Roll up the napkins and tie a bow around each one with the ribbon strips.

Use seasonal vegetables as table centrepieces. A big bowl of lemons or aubergines looks so pretty in the centre of a table (and you can use the vegetables afterwards too).

In summer, put tea-lights inside jam and Kilner jars. They look so pretty and you can place them around the patio or garden – such an inexpensive way of creating a great atmosphere.

In winter, snip off some sprigs of rosemary or thyme in your garden and place them in colourful glasses. Line these up along the centre of the table. Not only do they look beautiful, but they smell wonderful too!

apéritifs

Having friends around for a party is such a fun thing to do and it really doesn't have to be stressful at all. I remember the first time I threw a New Year's Eve party, I must have changed the menu at least a thousand times. Now, I just want everyone to enjoy the food and relax.

With a little planning, some helpful tips and simple recipes, your party will be wonderful. Dips and platters are a fabulous (and super-easy!) way to present food at a party because you can have them all prepared the day before with just the pitta crisps for dipping to roast off before guests arrive. Try making my recipe for Warming Cottage Pie (see page 141) or smaller versions of my Homemade Feta and Sun-dried Tomato Sausages (see page 150) and roasting them in the oven – these are the pinnacle of comfort food and will be sure to warm the hearts of your hungry guests. You can also make individual pies in ramekins, which can be made the night before.

A line of the delicious Lemon Meringue Angels in this chapter served in shot glasses on a tray is so beautiful and the best part is that they can also be prepared the night before and left to wait in the fridge for their grand entrance. This leaves you ample time to have a lovely, relaxing bubble bath, enjoying one of the many cocktails you'll find over the next few pages, before slipping into your best number. It is after all your party!

torino mojito!

This is my favourite cocktail to drink in the summer. It's so full of delicious zesty flavours. It is a fantastic cocktail for parties.

makes 1

2 limes, sliced into thin wedges
5 sprigs of fresh mint, plus one extra for decoration
2 teaspoons sugar
crushed ice
65ml white rum
splash of soda water, to taste

Put the limes (holding back 3 wedges for decoration), mint and sugar in a sturdy glass and mash so that all the juices in the limes and mint are released.

Add the ice, white rum and a splash of soda water.

Mix well and decorate with wedges of lime and a sprig of fresh mint.

Every time I visit Paris, I head for the wonderful George V Hotel before or after dinner for their champagne cocktail. So, here's a taste of my favourite cocktail in Paris...!

makes 1

george v champagne cocktail

cook's tip

making sweet salted almonds

Take 1 cup of blanched whole almonds, 1 teaspoon of butter, 1 teaspoon of coarse sea salt and 2 teaspoons of maple syrup. Place all the ingredients in a large bowl and mix well. Spread the coated almonds on a baking tray and toast in a preheated oven at 200°C/gas mark 6 for about 10 minutes or until golden. Leave to cool.

1 sugar cube
2 dashes of Angostura bitters
100ml Champagne
15ml Cognac
1 orange, quartered

Soak the sugar cube in a champagne flute with the Angostura bitters.

Pour the champagne and cognac over the sugar and bitters.

Garnish with a quarter slice of orange.

pimm's for wimbledon

I adore drinking Pimm's in the summer. Fabulous to drink while watching Wimbledon, on a picnic or at a summer party.

makes 1 jug

1 part Pimm's
1 slice orange
1 slice lemon
2 slices cucumber
1 sliced strawberry
sprig of mint
ice cubes
3 parts lemonade

Pour the Pimm's into a large jug, followed by all of the fruit and the fresh mint.

Add the ice cubes and top up with the lemonade. Stir lightly, and serve.

sparkling sicilia

I had this delicious cocktail in Sicilia (Sicily, in southern Italy). Simply multiply the quantities to make a larger batch.

makes 1

100ml Prosecco
1 tablespoon Grand Marnier
25ml fresh orange juice
1 teaspoon caster sugar

Pour the Prosecco into a Champagne flute and mix in the Grand Marnier, fresh orange juice and sugar. Stir and serve.

sangria

I learned how to make this cocktail when I was a bartender one summer at the White Dog on Nantucket Island in the United States. For a plusher version, top it off with some champagne!

makes 1 jug

4 oranges
1 unwaxed lemon
1 bottle Pinot Noir or other light red wine
5 tablespoons caster sugar
ice cubes

Thinly slice 1 orange and the lemon.

Juice the 3 remaining oranges into a pitcher and add the wine and sugar. Stir well, then add the sliced fruit and chill.

Pack in a portable sealed jug and serve at the beach in glasses filled with ice.

negroni

While we were shooting this book in France, Francesco (the photographer's assistant) made this cocktail for the whole crew. Everyone loved the cocktail and poor Francesco was on full Negroni-making duties until the early hours!

makes 1

30ml Campari
30ml red Martini
30ml gin
4 ice cubes
slice of orange

Pour the Campari, red Martini and gin into a cocktail shaker, followed by the ice cubes, and shake well. Leave for 10 minutes to chill.

Serve in a large tumbler with a slice of orange.

i'll take a manhattan!

Nothing beats a real Manhattan!

makes 1

50ml bourbon
25ml sweet red vermouth
1 dash Angostura bitters
twist of orange zest, to garnish

Place the bourbon, vermouth and Angostura bitters into a large glass filled with ice, and stir well.

Strain into a cocktail glass and garnish with the orange twist.

baba ghanoush

This ticks all the boxes – zesty, sweet, creamy and spicy. It's super-delicious!

serves 4

1 tablespoon olive oil
2 garlic cloves, chopped
½ aubergine, cubed
30g sesame seeds
100g Greek yogurt
1 bunch of fresh coriander
juice of 1 lemon
sea salt and freshly ground black pepper

Place a frying pan over a medium heat and add the olive oil. Add the garlic cloves and aubergine, and fry for 7–8 minutes.

Transfer the garlic and aubergine to a food-processor. Add the sesame seeds, Greek yogurt, fresh coriander, lemon juice, salt and pepper, and blitz to a purée.

Transfer to a bowl and serve.

guacamole

This dip is delicious served with a big bowl of tortilla chips or my Spicy Pitta Crisps (see page 173).

serves 2

1 ripe avocado
1 garlic clove, crushed
2 tablespoons freshly squeezed lemon or lime juice
1 tablespoon extra virgin olive oil
1 tablespoon chopped fresh coriander
sea salt and freshly ground black pepper

Cut the avocado in half, remove the stone (keeping it for later) and scoop out the flesh. Mash with a fork, add the garlic, lemon or lime juice, olive oil and coriander, and mix well.

Season to taste with the salt and pepper, push the avocado stone into the guacamole and cover with clingfilm. Doing this will help the guacamole hold its green colour.

white bean dip

dukkah

salsa verde

spicy pitta crisps

Try adding some finely chopped fresh coriander to the mix because the colour looks great, but go easy on the cayenne pepper as it is quite hot.

serves 10

5 tablespoons olive oil
1 garlic clove, crushed
2 teaspoons cayenne pepper
10 pitta rounds (each 13cm in diameter)
sea salt and freshly ground black pepper

Preheat the oven to 180°C/gas mark 4.

Pour the olive oil, garlic and cayenne pepper into a large bowl and whisk together.

Cut the pitta rounds into wedges (6 wedges per piece of pitta bread) and put in the large bowl with the spicy oil. Stir well, making sure that the pitta wedges are thoroughly coated with the oil.

Place the pitta breads on a baking tray and bake in the oven for 15 minutes or until they are slightly crispy.

Serve the pitta crisps warm or cool with dips.

cook's tip

marinating olives

Put 200g of mixed green and black olives into a bowl. If the olives are in brine, drain and rinse them first. Toss with a generous amount of olive oil, the grated zest of 1 lemon, 1 teaspoon of dried red chilli flakes, 2 sprigs of rosemary (crushed), some sea salt and 1 garlic clove (thinly sliced). Leave to marinate, at least overnight.

dukkah dip

This is a delicious, spicy Egyptian dip that is so easy to make and incredibly light.

serves 10

100g sesame seeds
100g blanched almonds
50g coriander seeds
15g cumin seeds
150ml olive oil
pinch of sea salt and freshly ground
   black pepper

Toast all the seeds and almonds together in a hot dry pan. Keep stirring until fragrant, then leave to cool.

Once the seeds and almonds have cooled, grind them together with a good pinch of sea salt and freshly ground pepper.

Place the dukkah mix in a bowl and cover with the extra virgin olive oil.

salsa verde

This dip is delicious served with toasted focaccia bread or my Italian Rosemary Crispbreads (see page 88).

serves 4

1 tablespoon white wine vinegar
4 sprigs of fresh basil
sprig of parsley
2 garlic cloves, crushed
2 anchovy fillets, chopped
2 tablespoons capers
100ml extra virgin olive oil

Tear the basil leaves from the stems and put in a food-processor with the rest of the ingredients. Blend for 1 minute.

white bean dip

This dip can be made in minutes and is also great as the recipe is made up of storecupboard ingredients.

serves 10

2 x tins of cannellini beans
    (460g once drained and rinsed)
2 teaspoons paprika, plus a little
    extra for sprinkling
6 tablespoons extra virgin olive oil
juice of 2 lemons
2 garlic cloves, crushed (optional)
coarse sea salt and freshly
    ground black pepper

In a food-processor, combine the cannellini beans, paprika, olive oil, lemon juice and garlic (if using).

Whizz until you reach a smooth consistency.

Season with salt and pepper, and whizz again for 20 seconds.

Scoop the white-bean dip into a serving bowl and lightly sprinkle some paprika over the top.

Serve with Spicy Pitta Crisps (see page 173).

cook's tip

making devils-on-horseback

My all-time favourite Christmas party food is Devils-on-Horseback. They are so easy to prepare and extremely rich, tasty and indulgent. Just soak some prunes in brandy overnight, wrap each one in a piece of streaky bacon, and grill until the bacon is crisp. The sweetness and softness of the prunes works fantastically with the crisp saltiness of the bacon. Probably not the healthiest option, but it is Christmas after all!

pink hummus

You get a fabulous pink colour from the beetroot in this recipe and it makes the dip super healthy! If you don't like beetroot, just replace it with 100ml of Greek yogurt.

serves 10

2 fresh beetroot
2 garlic cloves
420g tin of chickpeas, drained
juice of 1 lemon
4 tablespoons olive oil
sea salt and freshly ground
  black pepper

To serve
pitta bread
sliced fennel
sliced carrots

Place both whole beetroot in a saucepan with a little water and bring to the boil. Cover with a lid and leave to cook for about 25 minutes. You can test to see if the beetroot are ready by pushing back the skins with your thumb – if the skins come off easily, then the beetroot are done.

Once the beetroot are cooked, peel off the skins and chop roughly.

Put the beetroot, garlic and chickpeas in a food-processor and whizz until well blended.

Add the lemon juice and olive oil through the feed tube to make a fairly coarse paste. Season with salt and pepper.

Spoon into a serving bowl and serve with the pitta, fennel and carrots.

fresh raita

Delicious served with my Spicy Pitta Crisps (see page 173).

serves 4

200ml Greek yogurt
½ cucumber, diced
1 teaspoon ground cumin
1 tablespoon chopped fresh mint
1 tablespoon chopped fresh coriander

Mix all of the ingredients together in a bowl.

zaalouk

I make this dip on my Moroccan course at my cookery school and it's one of my favourite dips. It is really delicious served with toasted slices of baguette.

serves 4

2 large aubergines
3 large tomatoes
100ml olive oil
2–3 garlic cloves, chopped
¼ teaspoon sweet paprika
juice of 1 lemon, to taste
  (less may be needed)
1 tablespoon chopped fresh coriander
sea salt
ground cumin, to dust

Preheat the oven to 180°C/gas mark 4.

Put the aubergines on a baking tray and bake for about 30 minutes until soft when pressed.

Put the tomatoes in an ovenproof dish with half of the oil and roast for about 5–10 minutes.

Remove both the aubergines and tomatoes from the oven and leave to cool.

Cut the aubergines in half, scoop out the flesh and chop to a pulp.

Skin the tomatoes, remove the seeds and chop the flesh to a pulp.

Heat the other half of the oil in a pan, add the garlic and fry (but don't colour). Add the tomatoes, aubergines and paprika, and fry gently for about 5–10 minutes, stirring regularly to stop the bottom scorching.

Add the lemon juice, coriander and salt to taste.

Pour into a bowl and dust with cumin. Eat either warm or at room temperature with some bread.

smoked salmon pâté

This pâté takes all of 5 minutes to make! It's a superb recipe...everyone loves it. You can substitute the smoked salmon for smoked mackerel if you wish.

serves 4

250g smoked salmon
100g cream cheese
50g crème fraîche
juice of 1 lemon
sea salt and freshly ground black pepper.

Place all the ingredients in a food-processor and whizz until you reach a smooth consistency.

Serve with pitta bread, crackers or crusty bread.

easy florentines

These are divine served as a sweet canapé or at the end of dinner with a coffee.

serves 10

100g good-quality dark chocolate
  (minimum 70% cocoa solids)
100g milk chocolate
100g white chocolate
15g flaked almonds
15g raisins
15g glacé cherries, sliced
15g glacéd oranges, sliced
15g glacéd limes or lemons, sliced

Melt the three types of chocolate very slowly in separate bowls, each suspended over a pan of simmering water.

Take teaspoons of the melted chocolates and spread each teaspoon onto sheets of silicone parchment to form even-sized discs.

Press one piece of each of the other ingredients into the melted chocolate, and put in a cool place to set.

little lemon meringue angels

These are the sweetest angels I've ever had the pleasure of eating! Make them even more angelic by making your lemon curd from scratch (see page 22 for the recipe).

serves 10

6 meringue nests (medium-sized)
200ml double cream
150ml lemon curd
grated zest of 1 lemon

Break the meringue nests into small pieces and place in a bowl.

Whip the cream until it forms soft peaks, and fold into the meringue pieces.

Fold the lemon curd into the cream and meringue mixture.

Using a spoon, fill 10 small glasses with the lemon meringue mixture and finish by grating over the lemon zest.

Place in a fridge to chill.

cook's tip

juicing lemons

Try massaging the lemons before juicing to loosen up the skin. This will release up to 50 per cent more juice from the lemon. And, don't discard used lemon skins; instead, pop them on the radiator and they will give off a delicate lemon scent as they warm up!

simple dinner party menus

Some of my fondest and most precious memories are of friends and family sharing a homemade meal across the dinner table in my home. Whether it is a celebration or an impromptu gathering, there is nothing better than sharing a cosy supper with the people you love. In fact, dinner parties really have become my favourite pastime!

While the thought of hosting a dinner party might be overwhelming, it really does not have to be. When you use ingredients that are fresh, local, seasonal and, of course, delicious, your work is nearly done in advance. I find that combining simple recipes with quality ingredients is a foolproof way of creating a fabulous meal.

After much thought, I have decided to break this chapter down into seasonal categories. I'm a great believer in staying true to the time of year, as each season is bursting with its own flavours. Tomatoes ripened in the summer sun taste divine, just as comforting casseroles with rich flavours embrace the winter. It's my aim to incorporate seasonal flavours and moods into each one of these dinner-party dishes, from the starter through to the dessert.

roasted asparagus with hollandaise sauce on toast

If you have locally grown organic asparagus and good-quality bread, this is possibly going to be one of the most delicious tastes you have ever experienced.

serves 4

16 asparagus spears
olive oil, for tossing and griddling
sea salt
8 slices of good-quality bread
  (white sourdough works best)

For the Hollandaise sauce
400g butter
10 egg yolks
juice of 2 lemons
sea salt and freshly ground black pepper

Toss the asparargus spears in a bowl with sea salt and some olive oil. If you have a griddle pan, then place it over a high heat with a dollop of olive oil. When the oil is hot, lie the asparagus spears on top and leave to cook for 3 minutes on each side. If you don't have a griddle pan, fill a saucepan about one-third full with water and place over a high heat. When the water begins to boil, drop in the asparagus and cook for about 4 minutes (the asparagus is cooked when you can pierce it with a sharp knife).

To make the Hollandaise sauce, melt the butter in a saucepan. While the butter is melting, pour the egg yolks and lemon juice into a food-processor. On a medium speed, slowly pour in the melted butter through the nozzle until all the butter is whizzed in with the egg yolks and the sauce has a thick consistency.

Toast 8 slices of bread and assemble them on a large platter. Place asparagus spears on the platter and season with salt and pepper. Pour the Hollandaise sauce into a bowl and add to the platter.

---

cook's tip

other dinner-party sauces using hollandaise

For a Creamy Spinach Sauce, blanch a fistful of fresh spinach in boiling water, drain, chop and stir into a Hollandaise sauce.

For a Béarnaise sauce, cook some white wine or vinegar, diced shallots, tarragon and peppercorns together in a saucepan, reduce, sieve and then add to a Hollandaise sauce.

baked sole with salsa verde

This is one of the simplest ways of cooking fish and, if your fish is spankingly fresh, there is no better way to cook a flat fish in my very humble opinion...The salsa verde is fabulous drizzled over baked fish, but equally good served with grilled chicken or as a dip with vegetable cruditées. It's a great stand-by sauce or dip because it will last for up to 2 weeks in the fridge.

serves 4

1 whole sole, approx. 2kg
sea salt

Preheat the oven to 200°C/gas mark 6.

Score the flesh of the sole quite deeply on both sides, diagonally at 5cm intervals. Season well with salt and place the sole pale-skin-side down in a large roasting tin.

Pour in enough water to immerse half of the fish. Bake in the oven for 30 minutes or until the flesh of the fish is cooked. When cooked, the flesh will be white and come away from the bone with ease.

Once the sole is cooked, take from the oven and carefully remove the skin.

Serve with the Salsa Verde (see page 174).

Place the fish fillets on a serving dish and spoon over the Salsa Verde before serving.

lemon sorbet

These are so simple to make – it's just a matter of squeezing, stirring and freezing! They look so fabulous in their frozen lemon cups. If you don't have the time to make the sorbet, then just fill the cups with good ice cream and serve.

serves 4

300g caster sugar
400ml water
juice of 6 lemons (cut the lemons in half through the centre)
grated zest of 2 lemons

Pour the sugar and water into a saucepan and place over a medium heat. Bring to the boil, stirring every few minutes until all the sugar has dissolved.

Take off the heat and stir in the lemon juice and zest.

Pour into a large plastic container and leave to cool.

Once cooled, put the sorbet in a freezer, stirring every 30 minutes so that no large ice crystals form.

While the sorbet is setting, scoop out the fibres from the halved lemons and slice off just enough of the bottoms of the lemons so that they will stand upright. Pop in the freezer.

Once the sorbet has set, scoop into the frozen lemon cups and serve straight away.

roasted tomato and basil soup

I came up with this recipe when I was living in Italy. The base of the soup also makes the perfect topping for a bruschetta; just follow the recipe up until the point of adding the stock. Then, serve cold over toasted sourdough bread that's been brushed with olive oil.

serves 4

600g cherry tomatoes, halved
2 garlic cloves, crushed
1 red onion, chopped into large chunks
extra virgin olive oil, for drizzling
1 tablespoon balsamic vinegar
10 fresh basil leaves, torn
500ml chicken or vegetable stock
sea salt and freshly ground black pepper

Preheat the oven to 160°C/gas mark 3.

Put the tomatoes, garlic and onion in an ovenproof dish, season with salt and pepper, and drizzle with olive oil and balsamic vinegar.

Using clean hands, massage all the ingredients together for 5 minutes to enhance the flavour of the soup. Roast in the oven for 20 minutes.

Allow the tomatoes to cool slightly once they have come out of the oven, then tip them into a large bowl with the fresh basil leaves. Allow the basil to infuse the tomatoes. I usually do this for about 1 minute.

Pour the chicken stock into a saucepan, stir in the tomatoes and basil and place over a low heat for 20 minutes.

To serve, place a piece of toasted baguette on top with melted Parmesan cheese.

spicy crab linguine

This recipe is so light and refreshing. I love eating it in the summer. It's fantastic if you can get fresh crab, but there are also lots of great companies selling vacuum-packed cooked crab.

serves 4

600g linguine
olive oil, for frying
1 spring onion, finely sliced
1 red chilli, finely chopped
300g cooked crab meat
grated zest and juice of 1 lemon
bunch of fresh coriander,
  roughly chopped

Put the linguine in a large saucepan of salted boiling water. Stir for a minute, leave to cook for a further 5 minutes, and then drain.

Meanwhile, place a large frying pan over a medium heat and pour in a dollop of olive oil. Stir in the spring onions and chilli, and leave to simmer for 3 minutes.

Tip the cooked crab into the pan with the chilli and spring onions.

Pour over the lemon juice, stir and allow to cook for 2–3 minutes. Fold in the linguine.

Season with salt and pepper, and transfer to a serving dish.

Sprinkle the lemon zest and fresh coriander over the dish before serving.

rosewater jellies

Bring back the jellies! They look and taste so decadent. They tick all my boxes – easy to make, delicious, cheap and old-fashioned.

serves 4

For the crystallised rose petals
1 egg white
2 teaspoons water
12 rose petals (3 for each serving)
50g caster sugar

For the jellies
250g caster sugar
500ml boiling water
approx. 15g leaf gelatine
50ml rosewater

To make the crystallised rose petals, mix the egg white and water together in a small bowl. Grip the petals with a pair of tweezers and carefully dip the petals into the egg mixture, lightly coating both sides.

Dip the rose petals very lightly in the caster sugar and transfer to a wire rack. Leave the petals to dry overnight or for about 6 hours.

To make the jelly, stir the sugar and boiling water together in a saucepan. Keep stirring until the sugar has dissolved, then remove from the heat.

Pop the gelatine leaves into a bowl of cold water for 1 minute or until soft, drain and stir into the syrup until dissolved.

Stir in the rosewater and leave to cool. Pour the cooled jelly syrup into 4 individual glasses and pop into the fridge to set (this takes about 1 hour).

Arrange 3 crystallised rose petals on each glass of set jelly, and serve.

variation

Put 3 raspberries in each of the 4 glasses and pour the jelly syrup half way up the glass. Put in the fridge to set and then put another 3 raspberries on top, followed by more syrup, until the glasses are full. Leave to set as above.

---

cook's tip

making some crystallised flowers

All these flowers can be crystallised and then used to decorate cakes and jellies: daisies, nasturtiums, scented geranium leaves, lavender, marigolds, pansies, roses, calendulas, cornflowers and violets.

wild mushroom, parmesan and rocket bruschetta

There are lots of different toppings for a bruschetta, including the traditional tomato and basil (see page 188 for the recipe) or roasted asparagus and feta cheese.

serves 4

50g freshly grated Parmesan cheese
8 slices of sourdough bread
400g mixed wild mushrooms (such as ceps, oyster, chanterelle and morel)
juice of ½ lemon
olive oil
sea salt and freshly ground black pepper

Place a frying pan over a medium heat and drizzle in some olive oil. When the oil is hot, tip in the mushrooms, season with salt and pepper, and squeeze over the lemon juice. Allow to cook for 3–5 minutes, tossing all the time.

Toast the sourdough bread on both sides and drizzle over a little olive oil.

When the mushrooms are cooked, divide them between the 8 slices of toasted bread.

Place slivers of Parmesan cheese over the mushrooms (I find that my vegetable peeler is the best utensil for this).

italian beef stew

This is a great dish to serve when you are cooking for more than two people. It tastes even better when you cook it the day before. It's delicious served with olive roast potatoes (see my recipe for Lemon and Thyme Roasties on page 87) and just replace the lemon and thyme with 80g of chopped black olives.

serves 6

2 tablespoons olive oil
1 onion, thinly sliced
2 garlic cloves, crushed
1 red pepper, deseeded and thinly sliced
1.5kg stewing beef, cut into chunks
200g fresh button mushrooms, sliced
200ml red wine
2 x 400g tins of chopped tomatoes
2 teaspoons finely chopped
   fresh rosemary
1 tablespoon plain flour
sea salt and freshly ground black pepper

Preheat the oven to 180°C/gas mark 4.

Place a casserole dish over a medium heat and add the olive oil, onion, garlic and red pepper. Cover and leave to sweat for 2–3 minutes.

Toss the chunks of beef in the flour, making sure they are thoroughly coated.

Remove the lid from the casserole dish, add the beef, season with salt and pepper, and brown the meat on all sides.

Tip in the sliced mushrooms and leave to cook for a further minute.

Pour the red wine into the casserole, and leave to simmer for 10 minutes.

Stir in the tomatoes and rosemary.

Cook in the oven for 1½ hours.

This tiramisù recipe is the best you'll taste. I became obsessed with finding a good tiramisù recipe when I lived in Turin. Often, when you eat it outside of Italy, it is soaked in Amaretto or other liqueurs but, on researching it, I found that the most authentic tiramisù is made without alcohol. The real foodies say it's about the combination of good coffee, the subtle flavour of the mascarpone and the velvet sprinkling of cocoa powder on top. It should be really light and the flavours pronounced – Italian food is all about being able to taste each individual flavour, rather than being bombarded by a strong alcoholic taste.

serves 6

tiramisù

3 egg yolks
80g caster sugar
450g mascarpone
  cheese
200ml strong coffee
  or espresso, cold
14 boudoir biscuits
150g cocoa powder

Using a hand-held whisk, beat the egg yolks and caster sugar together in a large bowl until pale and thick.

Add the mascarpone cheese and whisk slowly until the mixture is pale and smooth. Stir in 50ml of the coffee.

Dip half of the boudoir biscuits into the coffee mixture. Place equal amounts into the bottom of 4 glass coffee cups or small bowls. Alternatively, put the ingredients in a single glass bowl to make one large tiramisù.

Spoon over half the mascarpone mix and sprinkle with half the cocoa powder. Repeat with another layer of biscuits, mascarpone mix and cocoa powder.

Cover and refrigerate for 2 hours, then dust with cocoa powder before serving.

french onion soup with emmenthal toasties

The trick with this soup is to caramelise the onions very well because this is where all the flavour is coming from. The onions should be a dark golden colour before the stock is added.

serves 4

80g butter
drop of olive oil
800g onions, thinly sliced
2 garlic cloves, crushed
1 teaspoon sugar
100ml white wine
800ml good-quality beef stock
70g grated Emmenthal cheese
4 slices of baguette

Place a heavy-bottomed saucepan over a medium heat and add the butter and olive oil. Once melted, stir in the onions and garlic.

Stir in the sugar and leave the onions to sweat and then caramelise, stirring every few minutes until they become a deep golden colour.

Pour in the white wine and leave to simmer for 5 minutes before pouring in the beef stock. Leave to cook for 30 minutes.

Sprinkle the Emmenthal cheese on top of the slices of baguette and pop under a grill to melt.

Serve the onion soup in heated bowls and pop the toasted Emmenthal bread on top. Yum!

provençal chicken casserole

This is traditionally cooked using red wine, but I love the flavour of the white wine with the thyme and garlic. If you are going to use red wine, then add some black olives to the casserole. Either way, it's absolutely delicious!

serves 4

1 tablespoon olive oil
1 whole organic or freerange chicken,
  jointed into 8 pieces
4 garlic cloves, whole
16 shallots, peeled
400ml dry white wine
350ml chicken stock
bunch of fresh tarragon, roughly chopped
sea salt and freshly ground black pepper

Preheat the oven to 150°C/gas mark 2.

Place a casserole dish over a medium heat and add the olive oil. When the oil is hot, add the chicken pieces and brown lightly.

Add the garlic and shallots, season with salt and pepper, and leave to cook for a further minute.

Pour the wine over the chicken and leave to simmer for 10 minutes. Pour in the chicken stock.

Add the tarragon to the casserole, stir and cover.

Cook in the oven for 1½ hours.

chocolate and cardamom mousse cups

Make these up the night before and then that's one less thing to worry about... Use good-quality chocolate and serve the mousses in your prettiest glasses or cups, and you can't go wrong.

serves 4

200g good-quality dark chocolate (minimum 70% cocoa solids)
100ml single cream
4 eggs, separated
1 teaspoon caster sugar
½ teaspoon cardamom seeds

Break the chocolate into a glass bowl suspended over a saucepan of simmering water. Stir often to make sure that no lumps form.

Remove from the heat and stir in the cream, egg yolks, sugar and cardamom seeds.

In a clean bowl, whisk the egg whites until they form stiff peaks.

Fold the whisked eggs into the chocolate mixture.

Pour the chocolate mixture into individual glasses or cups and place in the fridge for 1 hour or until set.

variation
To make a raspberry or strawberry chocolate mousse, omit the cardamom and replace with 100g chopped fresh raspberries or strawberries.

cook's tip

serving mousses

Use espresso cups, martini glasses or china cups for serving your mousses in, to create a decadent look.

If you are serving mousses for a dinner party, then make them the night before so that you aren't stuck in the kitchen for hours!

homemade edible gifts

Finding a perfect gift for a friend or loved one that is both meaningful and well liked is no easy feat. On many occasions, I have tirelessly walked up and down the high street in search of that one perfect gift and, more often than not, I've returned home disappointed or even worse - giftless!

More recently, however, I have traded in the hours and expense of panicked gift shopping in favour of something I love - cooking - and I have to tell you that within your kitchen cupboards are the best gifts one could ever receive. What better gift can there be, for example, than giving homemade truffles to a chocolate-lover in a fabulously decorated box or some freshly made biscottis to complement a coffee-lover's morning coffee? The whole idea of making a gift from scratch is incredibly refreshing. I have always found that food, whether savoury or sweet, has a way of connecting people unlike any other gift you can find.

In this chapter I have given you some of my favourite edible gifts and some ideas on how to make them look beautiful. I hope this will not only inspire you, but will also make your life a little bit easier. The possibilities are endless and the results are priceless.

summer basil pesto

This is another great sauce to learn if you are new to cooking. Homemade basil pesto is incredibly versatile and greatly improves the taste and appearance of any number of dishes. It goes very well with fish, pasta and chicken. I also use it on salads, crostinis and even in soups. Best of all, it only takes a few minutes to make and will keep in the fridge for up to 3 weeks.

makes 200ml

110g fresh basil leaves
150ml extra virgin olive oil
2 garlic cloves
30g pine nuts
50g freshly grated Parmesan cheese
1 teaspoon sea salt

Whizz the basil leaves, olive oil, garlic, pine nuts, Parmesan cheese and salt in a food-processor.

And, that's it!

variations

Substitute the basil with coriander or parsley.

Add 50g of soft goats' cheese and replace the basil with coriander, and you have a deliciously creamy coriander pesto that is fantastic with chicken or pasta.

cook's tip

preparing your jars

Be sure to clean all containers thoroughly with soap and hot water before filling. Look for unusual bottles and jars and fill them with delicious homemade chutneys, jams and sauces.

autumn compote

There is a feel-good factor about autumn pickings: windfall apples, hedgerows laden with plump blackberries, a neighbour's tree weighed down with ripe pears. It isn't just because the produce is free. I think it's more primal than that. Very few of us hunt for our food anymore, or grow our own, but come autumn we can go gathering. There is little to compare with the satisfaction of eating a blackberry and apple pie made with fruit you picked yourself. This compote is the essence of autumn. It is delicious whirled through Greek yogurt or scooped over a scone with lashings of cream, but also fabulous served with roast pork.

makes 10x230ml jars

100g butter
750g apples, peeled, cored and cubed
100g caster sugar
1 vanilla pod, split
250g blackberries

Melt the butter in a stainless-steel saucepan. Add the apples, sugar and vanilla pod, and cook for about 20 minutes.

Just before taking the apples off the heat, stir in the blackberries and continue to cook for a further 5 minutes. The texture should be nice and thick; if not, cook for a further few minutes.

After removing the vanilla pod, transfer the mixture to a food-processor or blender, and blend for a few minutes.

Press the mixture through a sieve and store in sterilised jars in the fridge for up to 2 weeks.

cook's tip

blackberry foraging and freezing

When picking blackberries, choose the ones at the top, as they haven't had much contact with rodents! Rinse them gently in a colander and eat that day or the next. To freeze the blackberries, spread them out on a flat tray, cover with clingfilm and pop in the freezer.

chocolate pistachio truffles

Melt-in-the-mouth chocolate truffles. Now, who wouldn't want to receive these as a gift? There are so many variations, so this is a great recipe for making in large quantities as you can split the mixture and add different flavourings.

makes 14

200g good-quality dark chocolate (minimum 70% cocoa solids), broken into pieces
100ml double cream
150g pistachio nuts, finely chopped

Slowly melt the chocolate in a bowl suspended over a pan of simmering water until it is smooth and glossy.

Gently heat the cream in a heavy-based saucepan until warm.

Pour the warm cream onto the melted chocolate and mix well until fully incorporated.

Mix in 100g of the pistachio nuts. Set aside to cool and firm up (you can refrigerate the mixture to speed up the process if desired).

Once firm, take teaspoons of the mixture and roll into walnut-sized balls, then leave to set on a tray lined with greaseproof paper.

Once set, place another 50g of the finely chopped pistachio nuts in a bowl and roll the truffles in the nuts.

variations

There are so many variations for this recipe. Try replacing the pistachios with hazelnuts or nibbed almonds. To spice this up, replace the hazelnuts with 4 cardamon pods or 1 teaspoon of ground cinnamon. Also try adding 1 dessertspoon of bourbon, Grand Marnier, rum or the zest and juice of an orange.

vanilla fudge

Homemade fudge is so superior to the shop-bought version. You will need a jam thermometer for this recipe, but it's a good tool to have in the kitchen anyway and it isn't expensive.

makes 24

100ml milk
100ml cream
350g caster sugar
80g butter
1 teaspoon vanilla extract

Place the milk and cream in a heavy-based saucepan, add the sugar and butter, and bring to the boil over a medium heat.

When the mixture comes to the boil, reduce the heat and leave to simmer for 15 minutes. Remove from the heat and leave to cool.

The mixture needs to reach 'soft-ball' stage, which is at 115°C. Once this is reached, stir in the vanilla extract.

Beat the mixture with a whisk until it reaches a thick consistency. Pour the mixture into a greased tray and leave to set.

Cut into squares. Store in an airtight container for up to 2 weeks.

variations
Stir 80g of rum-soaked raisins into the mix for fudge with a richer flavour. For chocolate fudge, simply stir in 90g of melted good-quality chocolate. For both these variations, stir in the chocolate or raisins after you have simmered the fudge mix.

christmas cookie dough

Cookie dough makes a delicious and thoughtful gift all year round. Patterned wrapping paper, stationery and cheerful scraps of paper look so lovely wrapped around logs of cookie dough that have been bundled in waxed or greaseproof paper.

makes 3 rolls of cookie dough

250g butter, softened
120g caster sugar
300g plain flour
1 teaspoon baking powder
80g white chocolate
70g dried cranberries, chopped

Put the butter and sugar in a large bowl and cream together with a wooden spoon until pale in colour.

Sift the flour and baking powder, then add the white chocolate and dried cranberries. Bring the mixture together to form a dough.

Cut the dough in three. Roll each third into a sausage shape. Wrap in greaseproof paper, cover with another wrap of Christmas gift-wrapping paper and tie at both ends with some pretty ribbon.

Write a little note on a card to say that the cookies should be cut into 8 pieces and then cooked for 10–15 minutes in a preheated oven at 180°C/gas mark 4. The dough should be stored in the fridge and will keep for up to a week.

hot chocolate mix

This takes just minutes to make, so this is the perfect solution if you are under pressure but still want to make a gift. Just buy some pretty bags for the mix and tie each bag with a ribbon.

makes approx. 250g

125g good-quality cocoa powder
175g good-quality semi-sweet chocolate, chopped
50g sugar
1½ tablespoons ground cinnamon
1½ tablespoons pure vanilla extract
1 teaspoon ground nutmeg

Place all the ingredients in a food-processor and mix until powdery.

The mix will last for up to 6 months in an airtight container.

meringues

Add a teaspoon of rosewater, lavender water or orange blossom to the meringue mix while you are beating it. You can also try folding in 50g of finely chopped hazelnuts, chocolate drops, nibbed almonds or pistachios.

makes 32

4 egg whites
115g caster sugar
115g icing sugar

Preheat the oven to 110°C/gas mark ¼.

Line 2 baking trays with parchment paper (meringue can stick to greaseproof paper and foil).

Tip the egg whites into a large, clean mixing bowl (not plastic). Beat on medium speed with an electric hand whisk until the mixture resembles fluffy clouds and stands up in stiff peaks when the blades are lifted. Turn up the speed and start to add the caster sugar, a spoonful at a time.

Continue beating for 3–4 seconds between each addition. It's important to add the caster sugar slowly as it helps to prevent the meringue from 'weeping' later. However, don't over-beat. When ready, the mixture should be thick and glossy.

Sift a third of the icing sugar over the mixture, then gently fold it in with a big metal spoon or rubber spatula. Continue to sift and fold in the icing sugar a third at a time. Again, don't over-mix. The mixture should now look smooth and billowy.

Scoop up a tablespoonful of the mixture. Using another spoon, ease it onto the baking sheet to make an oval shape. Or, just drop them in rough rounds, if you prefer.

Bake in the oven for 1¼ hours until the meringues sound crisp when tapped underneath and are a pale coffee colour.

Leave to cool on the trays or a cooling rack. (The meringues will now keep in an airtight tin for up to 2 weeks or frozen for a month.)

orange and almond biscottis

These will keep for up to 2 weeks in an airtight container, so you can make them ahead of time. They are also delicious halved and then dipped in melted chocolate.

makes 36

250g plain flour
½ teaspoon baking powder
½ teaspoon bicarbonate of soda
115g unsalted butter, softened
150g caster sugar
2 large eggs
2 tablespoons grated orange zest
1 tablespoon orange juice
150g whole almonds

Preheat the oven to 180°C/gas mark 4.

Sift the flour, baking powder, bicarbonate of soda and salt into a large bowl, and mix well.

In a separate bowl, using an electric mixer on medium speed, cream together the butter and sugar until light and fluffy.

Beat in the eggs, one at a time, then tip in the orange zest and juice. Stir into the flour mixture and almonds until the dough comes together.

With floured hands, divide the dough in half. Shape each half into a log and place the logs on a baking tray with 7.5cm between them. Pat into 7.5cm wide loaves.

Bake in the oven for 30 minutes or until the dough is firm to the touch. Transfer the loaves to a cutting board. Leave the oven on.

Using a serrated knife, cut each loaf crosswise on the diagonal into 1cm slices.

Arrange the slices in one layer on a baking tray. Return to the oven and bake for 10 minutes. Turn the biscotti over and bake for a further 10 minutes.

Transfer the biscotti to wire racks to cool. Store in layers in an airtight container.

cook's tip

gift-wrapping cookies and biscuits

Put your homemade cookies or biscuits in coloured cupcake cases encircled with a matching ribbon. Put the filled cases in a see-through bag. String a card with a note of the recipe and a glittery initial of the recipient on a ribbon, and secure the bag with a bow. Gorgeous!

index

Acknowledgements

When you write a book it's like going on a journey, and lucky for me on my journey I met the most wonderful and inspiring people that have helped in small and large ways to make *Homemade* the book that I dreamed of once creating. My first thank you goes to the most creative, inspiring and energising lady in publishing, Kyle Cathie – thank you from the deepest part of my heart for taking on my dream of a book and making it a reality, you're an incredible woman. Alberto Peroli, who is and will always remain in my eyes the most fabulously talented photographer that I have ever had the pleasure to work with – how you manage to always capture what I ask is incredible, thank you for all the patience you give me. Polly Webb-Wilson, thank you so much for pouring all your creativity and calm energy into those 2 weeks we spent photographing Homemade in France. Mum, what can I say about my mum. Well she came with me to France where we shot the book and she cleaned and cooked and made sure everything ran smoothly, as well as being the in-house counsellor for those stressful times! A huge thanks and applaud to Mark Latter and Caroline West for their incredible graphic and editorial talent on making this book look so beautiful! And to Catharine Robertson at Kyle Cathie for your patience. To my agent and dear friend Noel Kelly, thank you endlessly for all your support and belief, what did I do without you! And of course Niamh Kirwan at NK Management, you have been a dream to work with. And lastly but by no means least my two rocks: Judith Kelly for being such a wonderful colleague and best friend, and Peter Gaynor for giving me so much love and support.